MW01061968

"Oblates who follow Kardong on
see fresh ways to be shaped for C
the wisdom and guidance of Bene
of the Rule of Benedict, with thei̤ ̤̤̤̤
reading the rest of the Rule, Kardong shows oblates that the Rule is
not merely a historic document that looks backwards to another time.
Rather, Benedict is a way forward for people in their daily lives to be
the face of love through obedience, honor, reverence, and joy in their
own communities and relationships."

> —The Very Reverend Mark Strobel, OblSB
> Oblate, Saint John's Abbey, Collegeville, Minnesota
> Dean, Gethsemane Episcopal Cathedral, Fargo, North Dakota

"The subtitle of Terrence Kardong's brief collection of essays, *Reading
the Rule in the Twenty-First Century*, does not mean that the author
writes in emoji. It does mean that this thoroughly American Benedictine
scholar, like a high-res audio technician, lets the clear tone of Benedict
himself stand out from the many other voices that Benedict allowed to
coexist in his sixth-century Rule. Kardong has distilled and presented
a lifetime of rigorous scholarship in crisp prose—not lacking, though,
verbal emoji winks, grimaces, and shrugs."

> —Mark A. Scott, OCSO
> Abbot of New Melleray

"With his characteristic humor and deep, precise scholarship,
Terrence Kardong weaves a fascinating and unique look at the Rule of
St. Benedict in *Benedict Backwards*. He manages to do what one might
think is impossible after so many years of Benedictine scholarship:
he casts a fresh light on Benedict's Rule that forces one to confront
and engage it from a new perspective. *Benedict Backwards* is both a
delight and a challenge to read for twenty-first-century followers of
St. Benedict. This is a book that will definitely make a deep impact on
Benedictine life in the future."

> —Reverend Jamie Parsley, OblSB
> Oblate, Saint John's Abbey, Collegeville, Minnesota
> Priest at St. Stephen's Episcopal Church, Fargo, North Dakota

BENEDICT BACKWARDS

Reading the Rule
in the Twenty-First Century

Terrence G. Kardong, OSB

LITURGICAL PRESS
Collegeville, Minnesota

www.litpress.org

Cover design and photo by Monica Bokinskie.
Sculpture by David Paul Lange, OSB.

1   2   3   4   5   6   7   8   9

ISBN 978-0-8146-4618-2   978-0-8146-4642-7 (e-book)

Contents

Introduction

A title such as mine obviously needs some introduction, not to say explanation. Why do *Benedict Backwards*? What does that mean? Well, I certainly don't plan to turn the Rule upside down, but nevertheless, I do propose to read it somewhat from back to front. Why? Because I believe that it makes more sense to do it that way.

To understand what I am getting at, we need to understand that the Rule of Benedict (RB) is not a homogeneous document. By that, I mean that it is not all of one piece. The author almost certainly did not sit down and write it all at one time. Most likely, it was written over a fairly long period of time and probably as the result of lived experience. Furthermore, different parts of the Rule exhibit different influences.

Concretely speaking, the Rule of Benedict is by no means a totally original document. This statement itself would have been fairly shocking fifty years ago. We used to consider Saint Benedict the greatest of monastic legislators. He was often extolled as someone who succeeded in creating a new synthesis of earlier monastic Rules and doing so in a manner that people found especially attractive and practical. Benedict was considered the greatest genius of monastic literature.

I don't mean to disparage Benedict or his Holy Rule. Recently, *Christian Century* magazine published a list of the ten greatest Christian documents after the Bible. This list had to cover two thousand years of Christian history. I cannot announce that the Rule of Benedict was rated number one, but it was rated number two, right after the *Confessions* of St. Augustine! So it is generally considered a very great achievement.

Nevertheless, it is not particularly original. About the year 1950, just after the Second World War, European scholars began to suggest that Benedict probably lifted a good part of his Rule from an earlier document called the Rule of the Master (RM). As a matter of fact, the first ten or so chapters of these two rules are almost identical. They are not *perfectly identical*: someone has made some slight changes. But they are so close that one rule must be copied from the other.

Actually, we have known this for centuries. In the ninth century Benedict of Aniane already included the *Regula Magistri* in his collection of early monastic rules called *Codex Regularum*. A glance at the first chapters of RM immediately shows how close it is to Benedict's Rule. What should we make of this? Early scholars of these matters concluded that the RM must be a later copy of Benedict's Rule. As such, it could therefore be safely ignored. Since there are only one or two manuscripts of RM, they were pretty sure that it had no influence.

To underscore how completely we ignored this document, I can recount my own experience. I myself went through monastic formation in the 1950s. We did not have any very sophisticated classes on the RB, but we had enough instruction; yet I can certainly state that we never heard the Rule of the Master mentioned. Basically, nobody had ever heard of it. And even when it began to attract some notice, it was almost inaccessible because the Latin was so difficult. It was not translated into English until the late 1970s!

But even then the Rule of the Master posed a particular problem. To put it bluntly, it is a very strange document. Indeed, it is so strange that people who knew that were quite upset to find out that most probably Benedict had been copying from it! What is so strange about it? Among many other things, the RM exhibits bizarre attitudes toward community life. For example, the abbot is an absolute monarch, the monks have no real say in the affairs of the community (indeed, they are considered dolts), and so forth.

Who proved that the RM is primary and the RB is secondary? A very great scholar by the name of Adalbert de Vogüé, a Benedictine of La Pierre qui Vire in France, who died recently. De Vogüé succeeded, by dint of painstaking literary sleuthing, to show which text came first. He wrote up his findings in a vast, technical commentary, which has only recently been rendered into English by an American nun, Sister Colleen Maura McGrane. The first large volume of that commentary is basically devoted to just this question: which came first?

At any rate, we can say that even though Benedict copies the RM, he closely does so for only the first seven chapters of his Rule. After that, he begins to launch out on his own. By the end of the RB, we find Benedict has broken free of the Master, and he is then essentially his own man. Hence, I consider the last chapters of RB to be most characteristic of Benedict and so I stress them rather than the first chapters. That is where I get my title: *Benedict Backwards*.

Having said that, I would hasten to add that I do not apply this method in any rigid fashion. Generally speaking, the last chapters of RB put more emphasis on community than one finds earlier in the document. But that does not mean there is nothing on community in the first part. The Rule of the Master is supposedly about cenobitic life, as is the Rule of Benedict. But it has to be said that the Master has some very strange ideas about community life. Indeed, some of his arrangements for life together are so ill-conceived that I am convinced no monastic community ever lived by them.

Why, then, did Benedict choose to follow the Master in his first chapters? I must confess I do not know the answer to that question. In a sense, it is the "$64 question" of RB studies! Personally, I feel that Benedict would have been much better off working apart from the Master from the first word onward. But he did not, and that is the fact. At times, this presents Benedict with considerable problems, but somehow he always seems to overcome them. In one of the following essays, I will attempt to describe one of Benedict's rather amazing feats of avoiding disastrous ideas in the RM.

At this point, let me make a comment on the history of RB commentaries. In general, I find they put too much emphasis on the first seven chapters. I suppose this is natural, since a commentator usually begins at the beginning, and they are the beginning of the document. But then we often find that the commentator spends too much time and effort on the beginning. When he or she comes to the end, it seems he or she has run out of steam. This is certainly the case with the famous six-volume commentary of Adalbert de Vogüé!

But this is really no accident. As a matter of fact, de Vogüé, and many others like him, greatly *prefer* the first chapters of the RB.

With them it is a matter of choice, not chance, as it seems to be with Benedict, that the beginning is given so much stress. In my own commentary (*Benedict's Rule*, 1996), I tried very hard not to fall into this particular interpretive pit. And in my classes in the monastery, I actually treated of the RB starting with the last chapters first. So it was literally "Benedict Backwards."

Is there anything good to say about the Rule of the Master? Yes, there is. RM is a very full account of monastic community life. When I say "full," I mean it literally. In terms of sheer volume, the RM is three times longer than the RB, and it is also by far the longest of all the ancient monastic rules. That in itself is no great thing, but the Master also gives a rather complete description of what is needed to structure communal life. Compared to most of the other ancient rules, and there are dozens of them, the RM manages to develop the offices and procedures that have become standard in most monasteries down to our own day. Thus, the Master has a procurator, a prior, deans, and so forth. Benedict got most of his structure from this Rule, so we have that to be thankful for.

From the point of view of the scholar and commentator like me, I can also say that the Rule of the Master is a sort of Godsend. That is because it presents us with a very convenient foil against which to compare the Rule of Benedict. The word "compare" is crucial here. Without something to compare, it is often difficult or impossible to achieve an "angle" on a literary document. In many cases, we can easily see how Benedict has used the RM, or perhaps avoided it, or even contradicted it.

Of course, Benedict knew and used many, many other earlier documents. His favorite monastic authors were Cassian, Augustine, and Basil, but there are many more as well. A perusal of the index of any modern scholarly version of the RB shows that Benedict was a very well-read man. He must have had a good library to work from, and he used it very judiciously. To study RB through its sources is one of the most fruitful methods of appreciating the author and his monastic Rule.

Notice, please, that this does not detract from his literary excellence! Unlike our own time, writers in ancient times put little emphasis on originality. We should remember that the author of an ancient monastic rule was not trying to create a literary masterpiece. He was crafting a practical document to guide and structure the life of a community. It was common practice to weld together bits and pieces from earlier rules that fit the author's needs at the time. Actually, medieval authors tended to use the RB in the same way—in combination with other monastic documents.

Of course, none of this suits the modern standards of plagiarism or lack thereof. In our day of term papers and scientific text citation, we do not appreciate an author who lifts material from another author without proper acknowledgment. But for the ancients, such copying bore no stigma at all. They felt no particular need to tell the reader whom they were quoting. They assumed everybody knew. At any rate, modern scholarship cannot operate by the same methods. We need to cite the source of our authors.

Before I finish this introduction, I might make a few comments on one more aspect of RB studies. Given the now-accepted notion that Benedict sometimes copies the Master and sometimes basically repudiates him, this leaves the Rule of Benedict with a somewhat uneven appearance. For example, it means that at times Benedict, like the Master, seems to stress the individual, solitary monastic values. At other times, though, Benedict parts company with his basic source and stresses community life above all. This means that RB can have a sort of two-tone effect.

The eminent Australian Trappist writer Michael Casey once suggested that this composite quality of the RB may well contribute to its enduring validity. Casey said that this makes the RB "earthquake proof"! He meant that Benedict creates a broad enough basis of monastic life that it can withstand the strains and stresses of historical ups and downs. A practical example might be the recent willingness of some abbots to allow a few of their monks to live as hermits. The Rule itself always permitted that, but most abbots did not!

This, then, is a bit of background to explain my title *Benedict Backwards*. I certainly do not want to imply that I consider Benedict backwards! I agree with *Christian Century* that he is one of the greatest Christian writers. I hope my comments in what follows will bear that out. A final note: all translations in this book, with the exception of the biblical quotations, are my own.

Chapter 1

Mutual Obedience

Introduction

Since my general claim in this series is that Saint Benedict begins his Rule by emphasizing the individual aspects of spiritual and monastic life, the corollary is that the last part of the Rule is more communal, or, to use Benedict's sixth-century language, cenobitic.

To study the communal element, I propose to look at the concept of "mutual obedience." The term is bland enough, but let's consider what it actually means. At least in my understanding, it means that I should render respect and even deference, not just to those with authority and power over me, but also and especially to everyone I come in contact with.

This is an idea that permeates the New Testament. For example, in RB 72.4, Benedict, quoting St. Paul, puts it this way: "Let them strive to be the first to honor one another" (Rom 12:10). Notice that this honor is not just to be shown to the officials of the community, nor to those with more money or social power, but to everyone without exception. Put this way, it is a radical idea, and not at all something taken for granted by most people. In fact, when we look more closely, we find that Saint Benedict himself had a fairly hard time taking it on board!

What could I mean by that? In order to make my point, I intend to study RB 71 before lifting up RB 72. I want to do that because I think that RB 71 actually *fails* to cope with the idea of mutual obedience. In that sense, it seems, at least to me, to be a sort of first

1

try by Benedict to deal with this idea. But I don't think he succeeds! As such, then, RB 71 is an aborted first try at mutual obedience.

This kind of talk may not please all readers. As I found out when I published my commentary on the RB in 1996, some critics were rather offended by my remarks on this and a few other chapters. Who is this little monk who dares to criticize our Holy Father Saint Benedict? Of course, I was not surprised to meet with some of this kind of pious indignation. After all, Benedictines love their Holy Father and they also love the Rule he wrote.

But there is also such a thing as false piety, and sometimes that piety prevents us from seeing what is right in front of our eyes. The greatest RB scholar of modern times, Adalbert de Vogüé, said in his revolutionary commentary that the greatest obstacle he faced in writing it was the false piety of Benedictines who accused him of *lèse majesté*, that is, an insult to the king. In his opinion, the greatest favor we can do Saint Benedict is to read him carefully and then argue with him if we think we must.

RB 71: That They Should Obey One Another

The title of RB 71 is certainly promising. Benedict could not put it plainer: "that they should obey one another." He then goes on to spell it out in unmistakable language: "The blessing of obedience is not only something all the brothers should render to the abbot, but to each other as well." Clearly, he thinks that the idea of mutual obedience is not at all to be taken for granted. As a matter of fact, this is the first time that he has mentioned such an idea in the whole Rule. No, what the Rule has always emphasized is *hierarchical obedience*.

That fancy word means the lower gives obedience to the higher. In this case, the monks render obedience to their abbot. Every monk or nun who has been paying attention knows this: I must obey the superior! RB 5 rams that lesson home in almost violent language: no sooner is the order given than the subject must carry it out! (RB 5.1-9). This hierarchical obedience is well understood all over the world; no successful army, nor successful business, for that matter, can function without it.

The basic road to progress for the humble person is through prompt obedience. This is characteristic of those who hold Christ more precious than all else. For that reason, on account of the holy service they have professed, and because of the fear of hell and the glory of eternal life, as soon as something is commanded by the superior, they waste no time in executing it as if it were divinely commanded. (RB 5.1-5)

Of course, a monastery is not an army, nor is it a business. It is a Christian community that must run according to the distinctive ethos of the teachings of Jesus Christ. Now Jesus demands hierarchical obedience from his disciples: "He who hears you hears me" (Luke 10:16, RSV). In this verse, "hear" equals "obey." And there is also a triple hierarchy: Jesus himself obeys a higher authority, namely, his Father in heaven. For our part, we obey the Father by obeying Jesus. And the monk obeys Jesus when he obeys the superior.

Having said that, I want to add a caution: namely, the New Testament is not particularly focused on obedience to human authority. Soon after the time of Jesus, in the time of the early Christian church, hierarchical authority was not greatly stressed. The early Christians were all full of the Holy Spirit, so the leadership did not find it necessary to push people around. Of course, there were conflicts, but we get the impression that the earliest church was a gathering of equals, where higher and lower was not the point.

Getting back to RB 71, verse 2 makes a remarkably attractive case for mutual obedience: "For they know that they will go to God by this route of obedience." So Benedict wants us to understand that we don't just obey because that makes things run smoothly. No, we obey one another because it leads us to God. In other words, it is a "blessing" (*bonum*), as he says in 71.1, and not just a "labor," as he said in verse 2 of the Prologue. At any rate, these two verses make mutual obedience one of the greatest of all monastic, and Christian, values.

But then almost immediately, things begin to fall apart in RB 71. In verse 3, Benedict nervously interjects that "Therefore, except for the orders of the abbot, or the priors appointed by him, which we allow no private commands to override, all juniors must obey their seniors with every mark of loving attention." If we stare hard at this sentence, we see some remarkable things. First of all, it is introduced by the adverb "therefore." Now that is nothing surprising—except when we realize that it is completely out of place! Why? Because he then proceeds to qualify and even undermine what he just said!

Second, this qualifying sentence actually shifts ground considerably. It starts out insisting that obedience must be rendered to superiors, a principle we can easily accept. But then it immediately starts talking about the obedience juniors owe to seniors! That is quite a different matter, isn't it? Actually, this is not the first time Benedict has talked about that kind of obedience. In RB 63, he goes on at length about the seniority system in his monastery. It is pretty simple: the one who arrives at the door first is senior to one who arrives second.

Since most monasteries do not make much of this kind of seniority nowadays, it perhaps should be noted that it was once carried out quite strictly in most Benedictine monasteries. For example, when I was a junior monk, we even went to communion in strict seniority. Moreover, this kind of seniority had nothing to do with age. If an old man came to join the community, he could find himself junior to a youngster. That could cause some odd social dynamics, but at least it was basically fair since it undercut any kind of privilege due to wealth or social status.

Perhaps I should also add that hierarchy was a particular emphasis of the Late Antique society in which Benedict wrote. It soon developed into feudalism and then into the so-called "divine right of kings." But eventually it went too far, and it issued in the explosion of the French Revolution, which killed the king. And it would not be right to omit the fact that the rejection of hierarchy was one of the main causes of the American Revolution. The early Americans did not like kings and bishops! And some of this persists in our own mentality.

Benedict does not content himself with briefly stating the principle of seniority in RB 71; he carries it out to great lengths and really makes it into a strange and grotesque parody of true community. He says that if a junior offends a senior, he must instantly prostrate on the floor until the anger of the senior is pacified. I suppose that when we read such things, we automatically employ our commonsense filter and take it with a grain of salt. But let's take it seriously anyway.

Notice what it implies: here we have a senior monk who is so irascible that she or he inspires abject terror in a junior! What kind of Christian society is this? If this nun is really a senior, how come she is still in the grips of such anger? Is she not a contradiction in terms, this irascible monastic? You might say that anybody can get mad. Yes, but this isn't just momentary pique, this is an enduring rage, and apparently the senior cannot get over it. So the junior must cling to her feet!

Whose job is it to cure anger? Is it not the task of the one who has blown her or his top? We read nowadays of big-time athletes having a meltdown of this type, and what do they do with them? Send them to an "anger management" program! But in such a program the first thing you learn is that anger is *your* problem. The other person may be the occasion, but the anger is yours and you must deal with it. It is one of the principal, cardinal sins, and it must be forgiven by God. It is definitely *not* someone else's problem.

Benedict, however, shows no signs of understanding this, at least at this point. Indeed, he pushes on to the bitter end: if the junior refuses to make amends, he should be beaten, and if even that doesn't work, then throw him out! Expel him! Well, fine, but what about the senior? Who is going to teach her to deal with her anger? If a person is enough of a hell-raiser, people may get in the habit of just fleeing her. In a strictly hierarchical system, such a person may rarely or never hear the truth about themselves. But eventually, eventually, such a system cannot perdure. It must explode.

Before I close this part, I want to add a word to balance it up a bit. It is important to know who is the audience or target for this chapter. I am pretty sure it is the junior monk, not the senior. To fill out the teaching here, we should remember that seniors also have obligations toward juniors. Clearly, seniors must behave in a responsible and charitable way toward juniors!

RB 72: Mutual Obedience

At any rate, when we turn the page from RB 71 to RB 72, the contrast could not be greater. Chapter 72 begins with a strong statement about good and bad zeal, but it immediately explains that good zeal is in fact love (v. 3). Love is really the great theme of RB 72, but not just love in general. From verse 4 to verse 10, Benedict makes rather detailed and concrete points regarding love.

For example, 72.4: "They must strive to be the first to honor one another." Note first that this is a direct quote of Romans 12:10. It is in fact the only direct scriptural quote in the chapter, but a careful study reveals that the whole little chapter is saturated with biblical wisdom, and especially the special ethos of the Sermon on the Mount. The very idea of people running, really competing, to honor one another is hardly ordinary folk wisdom! No, it is the revolutionary wisdom of Jesus Christ!

When I first came to the monastery, we were reading an old translation of the Rule of St. Benedict in the dining room. This translation read: "They should prevent one another in honor." That struck me as basically ridiculous, even the antithesis of love. But a glance at the Latin shows that it was simply an archaic English version of *praeveniant*, which should be rendered "let them run ahead of each other to show honor." A very different picture indeed.

We live in a society that loves competition, but I believe that it can cause all kinds of problems, and I have tried to preach about it from the pulpit on occasion. Invariably I have visitors in the sacristy afterward telling me that I don't know what I am talking about. But consider: in competition, you have winners and losers. In fact, you have to have losers or the whole thing loses its edge. When we give everybody a prize, people feel something is fishy. But here St. Paul, and St. Benedict after him, seems to want everybody to be a winner.

Actually, this says a lot about the real spirit of RB 72: it is perfectly *egalitarian*. Now that is a mouthful, but it just means that everybody is perfectly equal. Of course, some are "more equal than others," at least when it comes to talent and virtue. But in the eyes of God, we are all his children and there is no hierarchy. Hierarchy, one above the other, is an invention of the medieval kings; but the New Testament is basically egalitarian. We are all equal.

A key word in this little verse is *invicem*, an adverb that means "toward one another." It seems pretty bland, but in fact it is absolutely crucial to the topic of community. Monastic community life is a life of mutuality. What really counts is how we treat one another, *invicem*. Here the noun is "honor": let honor be shown to all persons. It is not a typical modern expression; we would rather talk about love. But honor has a healthy stability about it. It depends not on emotion but on faith: I believe you are a child of God, therefore I honor you.

When we skip a verse and focus on verse 6, we may be surprised to find another holy competition: "They must compete with one another in obedience." Certainly the basic idea is much the same as in the previous verse. But now the topic is discussed in terms of obedience, not honor. This shows, I think, that the point is really the same; obedience can be discussed under different terminology, but there is no essential difference. Indeed, the literal translation of this Latin sentence would be: "Let them offer obedience to each other in an aggressive manner."

That sounds pretty strange, but *certatim* is not easy to render into English. The picture I get is again one of competition. But this is a very different competition! Normally people compete for the first place, but here they seem to be competing for the last place. Basically things are being stood on their head. This is by no means just ordinary common sense! This is not the way things usually work out. This is the revolutionary ethic of Chairman Jesus, translated into the cenobitic ethic of Chairman Benedict.

Perhaps in the back of our minds we can hear the echoes of a gospel verse. Remember Jesus' advice about behavior at banquets? "When you are invited, go and take the lowest place so that when the host comes to you, he may say: 'My friend, move up to a higher position'" (Luke 14:10, RSV). Jesus here supplies us with a sort of strategy of how to get ahead, but with Benedict there is no strategy: compete with one another obedience!

There is a curious discussion of this question in the Long Rules of Saint Basil. A group of monks or nuns tells the bishop they have a problem in their community: when they come together, everybody wants to take the last place. In fact, they are battling each other over the last place! How should these fundamentalists solve their problem? Basil says it is very simple: each one should take the place assigned to her. So obedience is again the key idea. But not obedience as each one sees it: obedience to the Gospel and the Rule.

One more verse in RB 72 seems especially applicable to the topic of mutual obedience. RB 72.7 reads: "No one should pursue what he judges advantageous to himself, but rather what benefits others." This is again very scriptural. It is a close paraphrase of Philippians 2:4. But when you consult that text in the normally accurate RSV version, what do you find? "Let each of you look not only to his own interests, but also to the interests of others." Notice the slight shift away from complete altruism to a sort of mitigated form of self-interest.

I will admit that the Greek admits of either interpretation. But I strongly suspect that the translator could not bring himself to give us the strong medicine of the pure altruism of Jesus Christ. The whole idea of putting the interests of others before my interests is so alien to our current approach to life that the RSV may have thought it was futile to ask that of people. At least let them consult *both* their own interests and those of others.

Granted, many psychologists would contend that in fact we mortals are basically incapable of pure altruism. We may think we are acting on behalf of others, but really we are always acting on behalf of ourselves. This is certainly not a silly or shallow point of view. It is essentially the view of St. Augustine and his famous doctrine of original sin. In other words, we find it very hard to overcome our basic selfishness. In computer language, we are hardwired to self-interest.

Rather than dig a deep hole here that I may not get out of, let me turn to another Latin term in this verse: *utile*. This may not look like a very interesting term: it just means "useful." It is an idea that everybody understands well enough. We should do what is useful to another rather than to ourselves. But I think it is quite possible that *utile* contains in itself the seeds of a deeper meaning. I would contend that it usually refers to what we might call the "common good." So then Benedict tells us to always act on behalf of the common good and not our own special, personal good.

Here we are reminded that RB 72 tries to present us with rather practical ideas about mutual love. We have seen that mutual obedience is one face of love. Now we are told that serving the common good is another face of love. It may seem to be a rather dry and abstract notion compared with the more highly charged idea of personal love, but it seems to me that it has tremendous significance, especially for monastic community life.

The idea of the common good does not get too much play in much Christian spirituality, but I think that is a shame. For whatever reasons, typical monastic spirituality seems focused on the question: "How can I become holy?" That is a perfectly good question, but I deny that it is the basic question of Jesus' ethic. For the early Christians, and for us, I think the primary question is "What do *you* need?" That is not necessarily contradictory to "How can I become holy?" but it is an important shift of perspective.

Then, to close these thoughts on mutual obedience, it seems to me that RB 72 really digs deeply into the question. Basically, it fulfills the promise of RB 71, which, for whatever reasons, got side-tracked. Now the issue is not hierarchy; now the issue is mutuality.

Chapter 2
Benedictine Leadership

This chapter will consider the nature of Benedictine leadership. It will be based on the texts of the Holy Rule, but it will also take into account our current attitude toward authority as well as its ordinary practice among us.

Benedict's Abbot

The main doctrinal chapter on the abbot in the Holy Rule comes very early, namely, RB 2. We might take this for granted, but when we compare it with a couple of Benedict's main sources, we find it is not typical of ancient monasticism. For example, both the Rule of St. Basil and that of St. Augustine discuss the superior only near the very end. Apparently they do not think the superior is the center of things. But the Rule of the Master, which is Benedict's main source for the first part of the Rule, does treat of the abbot in chapter 2, and the Master's abbot is absolutely paramount.

We can see that Benedict wants to provide his superior with a solid biblical foundation. In RB 2.2 he says: "He is believed to represent Christ in the monastery, for he is called by his name." How so? Well, he is called *abba*. Yes, but isn't *abba* the name for God the Father? In the early church, and Benedict still belongs to the early church, they called Christ *abba*. By this, they meant to say that Christ is our father in the spiritual life. We are baptized into him and only in him do we rise to new life.

When we stop and let this soak in for a moment, it is breathtaking, almost overwhelming. We are to think of our superior in the same way as Christ! Is that possible? What if he or she is full of faults? What if she or he is a weak person who cannot carry that much weight? Never mind. Benedict knows this. All superiors are unworthy, even though RB 2.1 says he is worthy of ruling a monastery. We are not in the realm of psychology here, we are in the realm of spiritual wisdom.

A quick reading of RB 2 shows that Benedict knows full well that this claim of high spiritual authority for the superior can be dangerous, so he surrounds it with hedges. For example, when he calls the superior *shepherd*, he implies that she or he does not *own* the sheep. "Let the abbot know that the shepherd will bear the blame if the owner of the 'sheep' finds them less than profitable" (RB 2.8). But immediately he turns around and warns the sheep that they are not just passive objects. If they do not follow their leader, the blame is theirs. They are free persons.

Chapter 2 on the abbot has high expectations of the superior. For example, it wants a person who can teach, but that's not enough. This teacher must also model. We have perhaps heard the current motto: "He can talk the talk, but he can't walk the walk." For Benedict, that's not acceptable. The abbot lives with the monks, and they can observe his daily way of life. If it contradicts his doctrine, he is a countersign and an obstacle. But of course, this puts a great deal of responsibility on the abbot. Can he bear it? Not without grace, he can't!

Benedict also wants a flexible and creative superior. "He should vary his approach according to the situation, mixing threats and enticements, now showing the sternness of a task master, and now the tender affection of a father" (RB 2.24). This is clearly a demanding job. It is not enough to be gentle, and it is not enough to be tough. One must be both. But the crucial thing is knowing *when* each approach is demanded and useful. Another name for that is *discernment*. It is a fairly rare gift, even rarer than flashier gifts such as golden speech or brilliant imagination.

RB 64: A Kinder, Gentler Picture of the Superior

Even though we indicated that RB 2 is by no means just authoritarian, nevertheless it could easily be read that way. And in fact, in certain historical periods, abbots and prioresses have tended to be rather hard and demanding. This often depends on the spirit of the age. In some ages, leadership was typically harsh and even cruel. In our own time, few communities will put up with that kind of martinet. It also seems that Benedict himself had second thoughts on his picture of the abbot.

In RB 64, he takes up the topic again, with rather different results. The chapter starts out by describing the method by which the superior is chosen. It is by election, which probably seems only logical to us because we live in a democratic society. But in fact, it was not at all "normal" through much of church history. Indeed, for much of the medieval period, even for a thousand years, *kings*, not abbots, built and ran the abbeys. They appointed one of their nobles as the "commendam abbot," mostly to siphon off the revenue.

But where the nuns or monks do elect their head, you expect something different, and in RB 64 you get it. The picture here is much more humane than in RB 2. Listen to this string of biblical images: "He should hate vices but love the brothers. When he must correct someone, he should act prudently and not overdo it. If he is too vigorous in removing the rust, he may break the vessel. Let him always be wary of his own brittleness, and remember not to break the bent reed" (RB 64.11-13).

These images are all drawn from the Old Testament, but they are also employed by St. Augustine in his various descriptions of church leadership. In fact, the whole tone of RB 64 is Augustinian, and it is intensely pastoral and humanitarian. Benedict is quite well aware that spiritual leadership has to be sensitive and gentle. If the spiritual leader hopes to accomplish anything in the pastoring of souls, she or he needs to remember that what is important here is not so much the relationship between the abbot and the monk as between the soul and God.

One time we had an abbatial election and a certain rather tough monk was elected. He had a reputation for efficiency but also ruthlessness. When one of my confreres was going out the door to return home to his parish, he said to me: "If he tries to run this place like General Motors, stand up on your hind legs and bark real loud." Well, I didn't need to do much barking in that case because apparently this man had learned a great deal when he was a minor superior. He was no longer authoritarian; he was consultative.

RB 3: Calling the Community to Consultation

One of the chapters in RB where this kind of consultative leadership is clearly presented is seen in RB 3: "Calling the Community for Counsel." Let me keep the spotlight on that last word: counsel. The topic in this chapter is not just corporate decision making, which can be done in different ways. It is consultation, in which the abbot asks the monks what they think about a certain issue. When they have expressed their opinions, he then takes them into account and makes the decision. It is not a classic democratic process.

Nowadays the church wants the monks to operate more democratically on certain very important issues. Canon law itself requires that there be a secret vote on the election of an abbot, on the acceptance of new members, and on the expenditure of large sums of money. Here the ballot, not the abbot, decides the question. This is plain and simple enough, although some communities do not like to be faced so squarely with a decision.

But Benedict's system is different. Here, the abbot is first of all a listener. He asks the monks to express their honest opinions and he listens carefully. Yet some abbots sometimes do not really care what the monks think, and they show it in their body language. One abbot took a consultative vote of us but prefaced it with remarks that indicated that he did not care what we thought about it. He already knew what he was going to do! Just to be contrary, we voted against him, but we knew it did not matter. This did not improve morale!

When we take a closer look at RB 3, we notice also that some of it is addressed to the nuns themselves. Benedict points out that they should be careful how they express their opinions in the chapter meeting. "The Sisters, however, should offer their advice with all deference and humility and not presume to assert their views in a bold manner" (RB 3.4). This may seem to contradict what Benedict has just said. This may almost look like a form of censorship, but I think it is not, for it simply reinforces the basic structure of the chapter meeting.

When Benedictines come together for chapter, they have to remember they are being asked for advice. They are not being asked to promote their cause. The chapter meeting is not a time for rabble-rousing or political speeches. We do not seek to convince the rest of the community of our opinion. We do not even try to convince the abbot. We just state our opinion simply and clearly. Then it is up to the abbot to make the final decision. For democratically trained and nurtured Americans, this may be a rather hard thing to swallow or even comprehend.

Years ago, when we rewrote the constitutions of our congregation, we made it clear that the abbot himself never has a vote in either the chapter or the small council proceedings. Some of the monks were indignant: how could we take away the superior's vote? It was quite obvious they did not understand RB 3. Consultation is just what it says: I ask you for your opinion and I ask everybody for their opinion—then I do what I think best. This is a rather subtle and delicate process. Some abbots actually ask for a lot of advice, but the monks may not be too happy with the outcome. Does he really listen? Was his mind already made up? Am I being taken seriously?

RB 5: Instant Obedience, No Judgment

To move from authority to obedience is to explore another facet of the same question. As with the previous material, it seems to me that the overall impression of Benedict's Rule is that he is quite strict about obedience. This impression comes largely from RB 5, which he derives mostly from the Rule of the Master (RM 7). Here is a typical passage of Benedict's chapter: "For that reason, on account of the holy service they have professed, and because of the fear of hell and the glory of eternal life, as soon as something is commanded by the superior, they waste no time in executing it as if it were divinely commanded" (RB 5.3-4).

There is no ambiguity in that, is there? When I say jump, you say how high? Instant obedience is known the world over as the proper response to authoritarian rule. Of course, it is the kind of thing that the army teaches, and it is also what we expect from dogs. In certain situations, the only kind of obedience that is appropriate is instantaneous. Moreover, a couple of verses later (5.8-9), Benedict spells this out in no uncertain terms. Instant means instant!

But a larger question lurks in the background: what has this got to do with religion and the spiritual life? Is it really suited to promote the kingdom of God? It may win battles, and it may produce obedient dogs, but can it really produce obedient monks? Surely monastic obedience must involve something deeper than just the automatic reflex of compliance. One gets the impression that Benedict, and the Master before him, has not thought this completely through.

There is something else that is even more troubling in this chapter. Consider verse 12: "That is why they do not wish to live by their own lights, obeying their own desires and wants. Rather, they prefer to walk according to the judgment and command of another." Now the issue is pushed further: they prefer to live by the will of another, not their own. How are we to interpret this? Actually, it is standard monastic doctrine: put aside self-will. And the way we do that is to heed the wishes of the superior.

But RB 5 itself may not be as hard-nosed as it seems. Notice that from verse 14 onward the focus shifts from instant obedience to glad and willing obedience. "It should be given gladly by disciples, for 'God loves a cheerful giver'" (5.16). This is quite different from military obedience, is it not? The army does not care much whether I *like* its commands. As long as I carry them out right now, that's enough. For Benedict, it seems, it is not enough. So the matter of obedience is at bottom a matter of the heart. Heartfelt obedience, not grudging.

RB 68: Questioning Obedience

There are some signs that Benedict eventually realized that his teaching on obedience needed some modification. In RB 68, we come across the curious case of a nun or monk who finds what she is told to do hard or impossible. Notice first of all, the title of the chapter: "If a Brother Is Told to Do Impossible Tasks." We might wonder right away what is going on here. Why should the superior give such a command?

John Cassian, somewhere in his massive collection of monastic writings called *Institutes* and *Conferences*, speaks of Egyptian spiritual masters who deliberately assigned their disciples impossible tasks. Why? Presumably to break their will, or at least to teach them humility. Thus a disciple was told to water a dead twig every day, knowing full well it was dead. But lo and behold, the twig blossomed after three years! Such is the power of obedience, says Cassian. It can work miracles.

Saint Benedict, however, does not think in these terms. When we read over RB 68 carefully, it becomes clear that the command is objectively possible; the impossibility is in the *mind* of the monk. But Benedict tells him that his first response should not be a sit-down strike or a loud protest. First, give it a try. In other words, one should exercise some monastic patience in the matter. This comes through in RB 68.2-3: "He should patiently point out to the superior why he cannot do it. He should do so at the proper time, and without pride, obstinacy, or refusal."

The Latin here is quite evocative: *non superbiendo aut resistendo vel contradicendo.* Allow me to quote my own commentary on these words: "The repetition of the *endo* form gives it the sonority of a big bell, tolling on and on. In itself, it is majestic and beautiful, but one must remember that Benedict is warning *against* this kind of steamroller approach to problems. It is not an obedient thing to overwhelm the superior by force of personality, persistence or in any other way" (*Benedict's Rule*, 569).

Anybody who has lived in a monastic community for a while realizes that monks and nuns must sometimes be asked and told to do hard things. There are tasks and duties that must be accomplished for the "good of the Order." We need strong-willed people to carry out these hard jobs: strong-willed people who are willing to submit their own wishes and desires for the good of others. This is the case in any healthy organization.

But it is not enough to say that the individual must sometimes be sacrificed for the good of the whole. Sometimes individuals find out who they are and what they can become only by acceding to the wishes and directives of the other. People with low self-esteem must sometimes be asked to do things they think they cannot do. Notice that chapter 68 ends up telling the monk: "If, after his suggestion, the superior does not change his mind or his order, the junior monk should realize it is in his best interest. Then, confident in the help of God, he must lovingly obey" (RB 68.5). It is worth pointing out that final adverb: "lovingly." None of this can be accomplished without love, and especially, none of it is possible without God's grace.

Chapter 3

Sharing Authority

In a democratic society such as ours, it is taken for granted that authority must be shared. At the most basic level, a single leader cannot attend to any large group; she needs help. But it is still not easy for some leaders to share their authority. Either their personality or their ideology prevents them from entrusting others with subordinate roles of leadership.

The Rule of the Master, from which Benedict drew much of his material, was written by one such individual. Whoever the Master is, he cannot share his authority. He is so jealous of his power that he keeps all other community members at arm's length. He may arrange for some lieutenants such as deans and cellarers, but he never gives them any real authority. They are mere functionaries: people who act as mere watchdogs and who themselves must always be watched. For his part, Benedict succeeds in breaking away from this lethal pattern.

The Prior: Benedict at His Worst

He does not, however, always rise to the challenge of sharing his authority, or at least doing so graciously. Probably the worst example of this failure is seen in RB 65, on the prior of the monastery. Anybody who has read over this chapter recognizes that this is Benedict at his worst. It is really one long rant from beginning to end. Nowadays, an alert editor would excise this chapter and tell him to try again. This is an embarrassment.

What is the problem? Benedict complains bitterly that some priors think they are abbots, so they must be slapped down, put in their place, even expelled! He goes on to say that the problem comes from the very process itself: if the abbot and prior are appointed by the same person, then it will be no surprise if the prior thinks he is equal to the abbot. Apparently, Benedict himself got caught in such a situation and he cannot get over it.

We can understand that such things can happen, but they need not happen. Curiously, we know from the papal records that Pope Gregory, that great champion of St. Benedict, the one who wrote the second book of the *Dialogues*—that very pope more than once appointed the abbot and the prior of the same monastery, on the same day! So either Gregory never read RB 65, or he did not take it very seriously.

In fact, the historical record does not back up Benedict's almost hysterical aversion to priors. Throughout most of monastic history, monasteries have had priors, and by and large they have worked out well. Common sense tells us why: abbots need help. A community of any size needs more than one superior, both because there are too many people needing attention and also because the abbot cannot be home all the time.

Although Benedict does not try to bolster this flawed chapter with biblical warrants, he does enunciate a principle in 65.13: "When the management is entrusted to many, no one person will grow proud." This is his reason for preferring the system of deans, but he does not seem to realize that it also undercuts the whole abbatial system! The monarchical abbot who tries to govern alone is a worse problem than the proud or ambitious dean. Of course, Benedict's horror at a power struggle in the monastery is understandable. Such grasping for power is the opposite of monastic humility. But the answer to such dangers is not to eliminate the delegation of authority as RB 65 tries to do.

The Deans: True Delegation

As we have noted, Benedict prefers deans. And indeed he has a chapter on deans, namely, RB 21. Historically speaking, we know that deans, that is, minor officials at the heads of tens (*decem*), existed from the very beginning of monasticism in the Pachomian communities of south Egypt. By the time of Benedict, two hundred years later, deans were no longer common, but he knew about them and he liked them.

RB 21 starts out very nicely: "If the community is large, let there be chosen from them brothers of good reputation and holy life, and let these be made deans. In all matters they should take care of their deaneries according to the commandments of God and the orders of their abbot. Only those should be chosen deans with whom the abbot can confidently share his burdens. They should not be chosen by rank but for the merit of their lives and the wisdom of their teaching." The chapter ends up threatening these deans if they do not live up to their high calling, but by and large it is a serene chapter.

If we take a look at the parallel chapter in the Rule of the Master, namely, RM 11, we find something very different. It is about ten times longer, and it is not serene. The Master's deans are hardly the same kind of people that Benedict wants. In fact, they are mere watchdogs. They do not need much personal merit or wisdom because their main job is surveillance. Sad to say, the author of the Rule of the Master is a paranoid character who is terrified of losing some of his authority.

It is worth reading the Rule of the Master just to get the full dose of this kind of fear in high places. This abbot does not dare to share any authority because he is so shaky in his own spiritual leadership. He absolutely does not trust other people, so he cannot risk allowing them any real authority in the community. In order to control everything, he has to watch everybody at all times lest they step out of line—or have an idea of their own.

The Bible contains a wonderful story that illustrates the folly of such fearful leadership. In Exodus 18, Moses' father-in-law observes him functioning as the community judge. People are beseeching him all day long. Jethro exclaims: "You are not acting wisely. You will surely wear yourself out, and not only yourself but also these people with you. The task is too heavy for you; you cannot do it alone" (Exod 18:17-18, NAB).

The solution to this case of overwhelmed authority is simple enough: appoint elders to help you with the minor cases. Reserve only the more difficult cases to yourself. But notice that this means trusting other people for good judgment. Choose people with good judgment and let them do their work. Intervene only when necessary. Trust, trust, trust. Distrust people only when they prove untrustworthy.

The Cellarer: Like the Father

Probably the strongest example of true delegation in the Rule of Benedict occurs in chapter 31 on the cellarer. This monastic official is often called the "business manager," which sounds somewhat pedestrian. But in fact, this official probably has the most authority in the whole Rule, apart from the abbot.

"The cellarer of the monastery should be chosen from the community. He should be a wise person, of mature character and well disciplined. He should not be gluttonous, arrogant, violent, unfair, stingy, or wasteful. Rather, he should be one who fears God and is like the father to the whole community" (RB 31.1-2). Somebody with a sharp ear or eye might think I have made a mistake in the last sentence. Should I not have said: "Like *a* father" not "like *the* father"?

Well, the Latin can admit of either interpretation since Latin has no articles. But no, I insist on "like *the* father." This obviously is a reference to the abbot, so it is a somewhat shocking statement. Do we really want a cellarer who is another father to the monks? Not exactly, but we do want a cellarer who has the qualities of the abbot. And this is quite clear from the fact that the list of things the cellarer should not be in the previous verse is lifted almost verbatim from RB 64 on the abbot. Plainly, Benedict wants the cellarer to be like the abbot.

Of course, this can have its problems. A cellarer who begins to operate as if he were the boss is intolerable. Benedict knows this full well, so RB 31 is also full of caveats. "Let him do nothing without the abbot's order, but carry out all that has been commanded" (31.4). In fact, the chapter is a bit overloaded with threats, but that is not unknown in the Holy Rule. Indeed, RB 2, on the abbot himself, is full of dire warnings if the abbot does not carry out his role in the fear of God.

Years ago in my monastery, we had an abbot who was an expert in finance. He had built a large priory in South America, and he had been the cellarer in the Benedictine headquarters in Rome. He was a first-class businessman. Taking this into account, one could pity anyone else who had to be cellarer in *his* monastery! Who would want him peering over his shoulder? But in fact he did not peer. He let the other man, who was also very competent in business matters, run his department. What went on between them, I do not know. But I never heard he was guilty of micromanagement.

RB 31 is in itself a very fine spiritual treatise. Take verse 7: "If some brother should demand something from him in an unreasonable way, he should not crush him with a rebuke, but deny the obnoxious petitioner in a reasonable and humble manner." This one verse contains a world of wisdom. Cenobitic monks are totally dependent on the community for their material needs, so at times they can get desperate. Some people are always afraid they will be left without what they need, and this can cause them to behave in a belligerent or even violent fashion. In these situations, the cellarer can be a lightning rod.

Perhaps we should add a few remarks about the relation of the cellarer to the abbot. A casual reading of a monastic rule like RB might give the impression that the author wishes to divide the authority in the monastery into the spiritual and the physical, with the abbot in charge of the former and the cellarer responsible for the latter. That seems to be the way that Greek monasticism divides the monastic authority, but it is not true for the Rule of Benedict. Here, the abbot is in charge of the whole monastic enterprise. He will probably need help in certain areas, like the business office, but he is still the ultimate authority.

Other Monastic Officials

The abbot needs other kinds of help as well. For example, there is the care and training of the new monks, nowadays called "monastic formation." Benedict has an extensive chapter on "The Procedure for Accepting New Brothers." Much of RB 58 appears hard to implement in modern terms, but the description of the novice director remains quite valid: "A senior should be assigned to them who is gifted in spiritual guidance and will observe them very carefully" (58.6).

The Latin phrase that I have translated as "gifted in spiritual guidance" is *aptus . . . ad lucrandas animas*. This intriguing expression could be rendered either as "gaining souls" or "causing souls to profit." If we choose the first, literal alternative, it may look like the director must win over resistant novices. This could be the case, but usually new recruits to the monastery come with much goodwill and openness. Yet they are still in need of someone who can help them find their true selves and the best way forward for them.

That is a good definition of all spiritual direction, but when it comes to the novitiate, it is all the more crucial. Because the monastic "system" is always somewhat confusing to the newcomer, there are many customs and procedures to be learned. This can take up a good deal of time and energy, but it should never be seen as the main issue in monastic formation. The main task of the novice is not to learn how to pour coffee properly or light candles, but rather to face herself and work at spiritual growth. That takes expert guidance and it is the real role of the novice director.

The second phrase applied to the novice director is "observe them very carefully." That looks straightforward enough, but it is also quite easy to misinterpret. Benedict's formation director is not primarily a spy! Since the novices usually live in close proximity to the director, it is quite possible for the director to observe almost every aspect of the novice's life. That is not only unnecessary but basically intolerable. People in our time feel a need for a good deal of privacy, and novices also have that right.

On the other hand, it is important not to confuse monastic formation with ordinary spiritual direction. People are normally free to reveal to their spiritual director what they choose to tell her. The novice is in a different position. The director sees things the novice may not want her to see. But in the monastic system, these things are also part of the way forward. In other words, I have to hear things about myself I may not want to hear. And the director may have to probe into areas of my spiritual life that I would prefer not to discuss. Obviously, the director must be a mature monk and not a nosy busybody.

There is, of course, another dimension to spiritual direction that has to be kept separate. The sacrament of reconciliation is not just spiritual direction. Here the penitent brings his sins to the confessor and lays them out for God's judgment and forgiveness. The minister of this sacrament is not expected to probe much into the person's life, and certainly not where he is not welcome. This is a different situation. Does Benedict address this sacramental transaction?

In RB 46.5-6, which is part of a short chapter titled "Those Who Err in Some Other Way," we read this: "If, however, it is a question of a hidden problem of conscience, he should only reveal it to the abbot or one of the spiritual seniors. For they know how to cure their own wounds and those of others, without divulging them in public." This is a powerful statement, but it does require some background.

For example, the idea that monks or nuns should be revealing their sins to the superior is by no means simple. In fact, the so-called "seal of confession" more or less prohibits such a revelation. If a monk confesses to the abbot something concerning the good of the community, such as an intention to murder a confrere or burn the place down, the abbot as confessor must not act on this knowledge. Thus the canon law prohibits such a confession "unless the subject himself requests it."

But it is not at all certain that Benedict was talking here about the sacrament of reconciliation. As a matter of fact, private, "auricular" confession did not exist at the time of Saint Benedict! The Irish monks were practicing it, and they brought the custom to Europe about a century after Benedict, but in his time in Italy, confession was essentially public. It was also rarely practiced and so the church soon adopted private confession.

Another point. It does appear here that Benedict wishes to share his or the abbot's spiritual authority and ministry. And so he speaks of "spiritual seniors" who are available to the monks for confession of sins. Although we may take it for granted, it is in fact a very significant arrangement, because it shows that Benedict wants spiritual authority to be shared. Granted, not every monk is a "spiritual senior," but clearly that lovely term does not apply only to the abbot.

Notice too what he says about spiritual seniors: "They know how to cure their own wounds and those of others, without divulging them in public." This is a gorgeous description of what we might call "spiritual discretion." Every part of it is important, but especially the idea that such a person knows that she herself is "wounded." Therefore, she is not prone to deal carelessly with the wounds of others. A spiritual senior is someone who has grown in the spiritual life but not someone who forgets that he himself is a sinner.

By this point we have seen that the Rule of Benedict has many roles of spiritual competence besides that of the abbot. The last one, the prior, is an unfortunate essay that reflects painful experience, probably for Benedict himself. It is best overlooked. But there are other monastic roles that Benedict handles much more positively and competently. In this he is totally unlike his predecessor, the Master. For Benedict, authority is not to be hoarded; it is to be shared.

Chapter 4
Choosing an Abbot

The Rule of the Master

The first six verses of RB 64 discuss the question of how to choose an abbot. The general method suggested is election, as in a democracy. This is not exactly the point, but before we get to Benedict's teaching, it is important to understand its context. If we accept de Vogüé's thesis that the basic model for the Rule of Benedict is the Rule of the Master, then we have to say that in this matter of choosing an abbot, Benedict has completely gone his own way.

The abbatial selection in the Rule of the Master is so different from Benedict's that the unprepared reader can hardly believe her own eyes. RM 93, which comes very close to the end of the document, is a huge (90 verse!) discussion of the method of choosing an abbot. The title itself settles the matter: "The installation of a new abbot chosen by his predecessor from among all." The key word here is "predecessor." There is no election here. This is a dynastic succession where the abbot personally selects his own successor.

This in itself does not seem unusual. We know from monastic history that the first cenobitic abbot, namely, Pachomius in Egypt, handpicked his own successor (see SBo, Veilleux, 121ff.). In this case, which occurred about two hundred years before the time of Benedict, the results were not very reassuring, but that is beside the point. What is clear is that the founder of the *koinonia* tried to make sure that his vision of monastic life would be carried on by the next leader.

The phenomenon of a monastic founder choosing his own successor must have something almost inevitable about it, since it has recurred often in monastic history. Moreover, when the Holy See is involved, it often appoints the successor. In fact, that recently seems to have happened again at the famous French monastery of Taizé, where the murdered founder, Brother Roger Schutz, was replaced by another brother, but no election was reported.

To get back to the Rule of the Master, RM 92–94 does not leave things vague but spells out the exact process whereby the abbot should choose his successor. He should carefully observe the monks to see which one is most qualified, that is, the most obedient. When he decides which one that is, he should publically designate him his successor. Then an elaborate ceremony is presented wherein this takes place. When the old abbot dies, the successor automatically takes his place.

Up to this point, we may not sense any great problem. But there are in fact serious flaws in this system. For example, the Master actually instructs the monks to *look obedient* in front of the abbot so that they might be chosen to succeed him. There is nothing subtle about this:

> So while the abbot sees all the brothers panting with thirst for this honor and each one competing to evince in himself works of holiness in what is good according to the precepts of God, he will continually be pondering in his mind and scrutinizing with his eyes which of them all stands out in the rivalry of observance as the most excellent and perfect. (RM 92.71-72, Eberle, 275)

Now all of this is supposed to happen when the abbot is on his last legs. But what happens if the abbot does not in fact die? Big trouble! He should watch the designated successor with an eagle eye, and if he shows the least signs of pride, depose him and humiliate him. Now all of this is very strange and, to use the correct word, an embarrassment. We should be grateful that Benedict had the good sense to avoid it.

Benedict's "System"

To turn to Benedict, he drastically abridges the whole discussion. From two hundred verses in the RM, he manages to discuss the question in six! He accomplishes this reduction by simply ignoring the Master's grotesque and manifestly unworkable system. RB 64.1-6 quietly drops the dynastic system of the Master for something quite different:

> In the installation of an abbot, the proper method is always to appoint the one whom the whole community agrees to choose in the fear of God. Or a part of the community, no matter how small, may make the choice if they possess sounder judgment. Let the candidate be chosen for merit of life and wisdom of teaching, even if he hold the last rank in the community.

Probably most of us find this approach to succession superior to that of the Master. Especially if we are the citizens of a modern democracy, we feel it is the proper way to approach the question of leadership. But let us look a little closer at what Benedict actually says.

Notice, for example, the innocent little phrase "in the fear of God." It is a biblical turn of speech, which hardly catches our eye. But if we let it do its intended work, it should pack a much stronger wallop. In our American experience, politics are not normally done "in the fear of God." People strive for office and for power, and "fear" of any kind is not expected from them. Indeed, when a candidate like, say, Edmund Muskie sheds a tear, he is immediately suspect as a wimp who is too weak to lead us.

The fear of God should characterize monastic transactions because, in fact, we are only gathered together to do God's work and to carry out his will. Yet Benedict, in RB 64.3-6, is acutely aware that not all monastic elections are actually carried out "in the fear of God." They may seem to be so on the surface, but in fact they are flawed. They are such either because the electors have the wrong motives or because the elected one has also accepted the choice for the wrong reasons. We will return to this problem further on.

What kind of person should be chosen? Not just the most obedient one, as the Master would have it, but "one chosen for merit of life and wisdom of teaching" (64.2). This is a rather terse job description, which we could and no doubt should expand. But it is still worth pondering a bit. Merit of life and wisdom of teaching trump mere obedience, because the latter is not sufficient in a leader. A leader has to be more, much more, than compliant and docile. Those qualities are acceptable in the average monk or nun, but not for the leader.

If the monastic community is too concerned to produce "yes-men," it may find itself faced with a perilous situation when it comes to an election. If all the candidates are basically docile and compliant, they may be ideal followers but not leaders. We sometimes hear that this is a situation that occurs in modern monasteries. When it comes time to find a new leader, no one qualifies because no one has leadership qualities. Even "merit of life and wisdom of teaching" may not be a sufficient guideline. What about courage? What about discretion? What about vision? These may be in short supply, but they are essential for monastic leadership.

Many years ago, in the context of a General Chapter, these same issues rose to the surface. The basic question was: "Should a monk *want* to be abbot?" This may seem like a strange and useless question, but it is not. In one sense, monastic humility may seem to rule out the monk who actually *wants* to be abbot. As one of my confreres put it once in a preelection sermon: "It is a catch 22: if you want to be abbot, you are thereby crazy. So you are disqualified."

Indeed, the situation may be even more complicated. One of the abbots present at the General Chapter commented that humility can undermine our whole election process. How so? Because the person who insists he does not want to be abbot, can, if he is still elected, always find a loophole by reminding the community that he never wanted to be abbot in the first place! And in fact, some abbots actually hold this kind of threat over the community. If you don't do what I want, I am quite ready to resign.

To return to RB 64, Benedict does not just tell the monks to elect one of their members. That would be clear and simple enough. But Benedict adds a qualifying proviso that is by no means clear and simple: "A part of the community, no matter how small, may make the choice if they possess sounder judgment" (64.1). Even if we think hard about this, we probably will not be able to sort it out. Who decides who has sounder judgment? There are many situations in life where such a method is the only practical one, but hardly in a small monastery.

The Catholic Church, which now carefully monitors monastic elections, certainly does not accept Benedict's proviso. A valid election must be done by secret ballot and every qualified elector must be allowed to vote. The method is strictly democratic: one man (woman), one vote. The majority determines the result. No subjectivity is allowed to play a part in this process. In fact, the papal conclave and the free election of religious superiors are the only real elections currently practiced in the Catholic Church.

All of this is controlled by canon law. One time the superior of the local convent called up our abbot and said that they were preparing to elect her successor. They held a "straw ballot" but one of the strongest candidates was only thirty-five years old. She felt that was too young, so she did not want to let her name go forward. The abbot called a canonist and passed on her problem. His answer was that not only must she not remove her name from the ballot; if she did, the entire election would be null and void. Canon law admits of no exceptions on this matter.

The History of Monastic Elections

Since Benedictine monks and nuns routinely elect their superiors more or less as Benedict instructed, we may assume they have always done so. But that is far from true! Over the long course of Benedictine history, real elections have probably been the exception, not the norm. Through much of the medieval period and right down to the end of the *ancient régime* about 1800, monastic superiors were appointed by higher-ups and not elected by the members. Benedict himself reacts rather violently against this practice in RB 65, but that did not stop it from taking place.

For example, we know from the official letters of Pope Gregory the Great that he himself often appointed abbots for the various monasteries of the Latin Church. Even though he expresses considerable admiration for the Holy Rule of Benedict, he does not seem to mind violating it on this point. Kassius Hallinger said that Pope Gregory probably did not actually know much about the Holy Rule! That is another issue.

But papal appointment was far from the worst aberration in this regard. For much of the medieval period, abbots and abbesses were chosen and installed by kings and princes. Free elections were exceedingly rare in monasteries from the sixth to the nineteenth century. Since the kings built the monasteries and funded them, they naturally felt it was their right to install a superior of their own choosing. This often involved a *commendam abbot*, that is, a layperson who then made sure to siphon off much of the monastic revenues. The actual local superior was the prior, but he was not elected either.

So, historically speaking, the current situation of free elections is a big improvement, and not to be taken for granted. Since we often hear that "the church is not a democracy," we should worry a bit what that might mean for us. Does it imply that therefore the church is a monarchy or an autocracy? Nobody has quite the nerve to claim that, but this constant denial that the church is a democracy shows that people are not comfortable with "one man, one vote." So therefore monks and nuns should jealously guard this part of their heritage.

Flaws in the System

The election system is good, but it is not perfect. For example, a monk must be a priest before he can be elected abbot. When our monasteries were strictly segregated between priests and brothers, this sort of qualification might have seemed logical. But since the Second Vatican Council, such distinctions have been abolished in our monasteries. There is now only one class of monk; whether one is ordained or not is no longer decisive—except in regard to the abbatial succession!

In practice, this means that a brother cannot be elected abbot. When a brother participates in an abbatial election, he has an "active vote," but not a "passive vote." That is, he can vote for abbot, but he cannot be voted for. If, for some reason, the monks persist in electing a brother for abbot, the Holy See will reply that so-and-so can be abbot, but he must first be ordained a priest. This shows that there are at least two important steps in the election: voting and confirmation.

What is the basis for this distinction? Why must the abbot be a priest? After all, the monastic realm and the ecclesial realm are different. Monks are technically laymen. Why must the superior be different? Rome has never issued an official explanation, but the usual assumption is that they do not want a brother to be superior over priests. This gets us into arcane canonical distinctions about jurisdiction and so forth.

Whatever the reasoning, it can cause problems for a given community. If a monastery finds itself with a shortage of priest-candidates, what is to be done? It may be that the best candidates are in fact brothers. Years ago, that was rarely the case because the brothers usually did not have enough education to function as abbot. But nowadays, some of the brothers are highly educated and also highly gifted in leadership. This seems like a false dilemma that only the Holy See can solve.

Final Musings

These ruminations on monastic elections may seem somewhat excessive, but in fact leadership is, and has always been, an extremely important issue in the church and the monastery. Without good leaders, communities do not flourish. Moreover, good leadership is a divine gift, without which "the people perish." Where adequate leadership is unavailable, the whole enterprise is in jeopardy.

For example, in the foundation of a new monastery in a different culture, it is not just enough that sufficient numbers of women or men take on the habit. It is also essential that native *leadership* emerges and takes hold. Indeed, if the foreign-based founding community continues to supply the leadership, it will inevitably be accused of "colonialism." Why hasn't leadership been transferred to the local community? Why has the founder not relinquished control? But what if the native monastics do not *want* to take over their own destiny?

Moreover, there is some evidence that the younger generation worldwide is not too eager to assume control of our monasteries. It has been observed of the so-called Generation X that the thing they most highly prize is smooth and harmonious human relations. But of course, the religious superior often finds that she must cope with conflict and disharmony. Then what? That is when it would be preferable to simply be a "humble monk" and avoid such troubles. But, as Harry Truman famously said, "The buck stops here!" Somebody must take the lead.

Of course, none of this happens in a vacuum. Monastic leadership always exists in a certain historical context. Now the current context in the postindustrial Western world is not particularly fond of strong leaders. In the pioneer days, conditions were tough—so tough that only a strong leader could overcome the obstacles. People in general needed considerable ego-strength to cope with life. This included monks. Chapter meetings were not necessarily characterized by excessive docility or humility.

Nowadays, the typical monastic leader knows that she or he will get further by gentle methods, not harshness. Not all of our leaders can find the right level of softness or toughness to please their subjects (or constituents). Of course, this is not a new problem. Down through history, kings had to learn the same lessons.

Chapter 5

Better Than Benedict?

Some years ago a German scholar by the name of Albrecht Diem wrote an article in which he lavished praise on an obscure seventh-century French monastic rule called "The Rule of a Certain Father for Virgins." Diem has studied this Rule in depth, and he claims that it is especially strong in its sense of community. And that in turn is based on what he calls the *diktat des Liebes*, the love commandment.

Having researched this same Rule myself, I can agree with Diem that the *Regula Cuiusdam* is indeed a fine monastic rule. But I cannot follow him when he goes on to say that he thinks this Rule is even superior to the Rule of Benedict: "This is a coherent and theologically differentiated monastic program that far exceeds its model (RB) in literary quality and theological depth, as well as the boldness of its communal ideal" (p. 85). This claim is almost shocking, since most historians give Benedict the highest place among the ancient monastic rules. And he is usually regarded as one of the greatest teachers on Christian community and mutual love.

So then, I am tempted to immediately jump to Benedict's defense, as Diem expects many scholars will do, for he is something of a *pro-vocateur*. Yet I must also admit that I am a bit hesitant to function as Benedict's champion. In one of his voluminous writings, Adalbert de Vogüé noted that too many Benedictine scholars have spent too much time defending Benedict, but sometimes their instincts blind them to some of his defects. Remember that the Rule is not Holy Scripture. It has its weak aspects.

Before I proceed, let me add that this *Regula Cuiusdam* was not entirely unknown in medieval Europe. For example, Benedict of Aniane compiled an anthology of earlier monastic rules about AD 800, and in it he gave this Rule for Nuns a high place. Indeed, he excerpted almost every chapter of it in his commentary on the Rule of Benedict called *Concordia Regularum*. Benedict of Aniane was a sophisticated connoisseur of fine rules, so this is a very precious endorsement.

Love Trumps All

To get a bit more specific, Diem says that, whereas love is the key value in the *Regula Cuiusdam*, this is not true for Benedict. For RB, he argues, the primary monastic values are *humility*, *obedience*, and *mortification*. Since Benedict never mentions *mortification*, we can leave this one aside, but there is no doubt that Benedict does put great stress on humility and obedience. Indeed, the first part of the Rule of Benedict includes a long, detailed chapter on humility (RB 7) and another powerful chapter on obedience (RB 5). There is another shorter chapter on silence, and these three monastic virtues form Benedict's "spiritual directory" as Adalbert de Vogüé puts it.

Now, as Diem insists, there is no doubt that for Christians of any sort, love is the primary value. The whole New Testament teaches precisely this: love is the heart of the Gospel of Jesus Christ. No Christian theologian will deny that. But then where do humility, obedience, and silence come in? In his three treatises found in RB 5–7, Benedict does base these virtues on biblical warrants, but we really cannot say they are the primary Christian virtues. So where did Benedict get them?

The answer to that is very simple: he got them from the Rule of the Master. Since about 1960, it has been pretty well accepted by scholars that Benedict is heavily dependent on this earlier Rule, and not vice-versa, as we used to think. Anyone who reads through the first ten chapters of the Rule of the Master can immediately see that it is almost word-for-word similar to Benedict's first seven chapters. As I pointed out in the introductory chapter, this means that this material is not Benedict's own; at least we can say that this is not where you find Benedict's most characteristic emphases.

But the fact remains that this is Benedict's *first* teaching, and for some readers it seems to be what most impresses them. For example, Adalbert de Vogüé, in his huge and very influential commentary on the RB, which is only now being translated into English, puts most of his emphasis on Benedict's first seven chapters. In fact, he wrote hundreds of pages on humility and obedience. But when he comes to the end of the Rule it is a different story. Then he can only manage a few rather perfunctory remarks on the last chapters. Remember that it is these last chapters that contain Benedict's main teaching on community life. Apparently, Albrecht Diem thinks about the Rule of Benedict in the same way: *first is most important.*

Cenobitism and Anchoritism

It is not only humility and obedience that tend to confuse the issues here. The same could be said about *anchoritism.* We are well aware that Benedict, in his first chapter, has a lot to say about hermits:

> The second kind of monks are the anchorites, that is, hermits. Their observance is no mere novice-fervor but the result of long testing in a monastery. Community support has taught them how to battle the devil, and this excellent training in the fraternal battle-line enables them to venture out to the single combat of the desert. There they are able to fight with God's help against vices of flesh and thought, relying on their own hand and arm rather than relying on the help of others.

Compared to this, Benedict's characterization of the cenobitic life is much less noteworthy: "The first kind of monks are the cenobites, who live in monasteries under a rule and an abbot" (RB 1.2). He does add later that these cenobites are the "strongest [*fortissimum*] kind of monks" (RB 1.13). But I would have to say that in RB 1, the hermits have the best of it. Isn't it strange, then, that Benedict *never* mentions the hermits again in the entire Rule? There is no doubt either that the Rule is written for cenobites, so I have to say that I find it rather unfortunate that Benedict has seen fit to lead off his Rule with such a chapter. Yet the reason is obvious: he is simply copying the Rule of the Master.

If you read any amount of the Rule of the Master, you have to come to the conclusion that for the Master, community is not a primary value at all. Indeed, it seems that his basic orientation is anchoritic. It is a commonplace now to say that the Master is mostly inspired by the thinking of the Desert Fathers, especially John Cassian. There is nothing wrong with that, but it has to be noted and stressed that the basic thinking of the Desert Fathers is not cenobitic. For them, the primary structure is not community; it is the master-disciple relation. In the Rule of the Master, what really counts is the nexus between the individual monk and the abbot. The relationship between the brothers means very little.

To come back to Albrecht Diem, it seems that he also takes RB 1 too seriously. To show how this is, I quote from his article: "While the *Regula Benedicti* only for pragmatic reasons recognizes the cenobitic life as the best way to salvation, the *Regula Cuiusdam* is totally sold on the monastic community life." The phrase that sticks out like a sore thumb here, at least for me, is this one: "only for pragmatic reasons." Standing alone, this could mean many things, but Diem makes it very specific in his footnote, where he cites RB 1.2-5 as an example of Benedict's "pragmatism."

When we look back over RB 1.2-5, it is pretty obvious what Diem means. He sees the cenobitic life as a preparatory stage for hermits. Now I must admit that when we take this passage in itself, it does look like that is what Benedict means. If community life is a kind of novitiate for the solitary monastic life, then it does look preparatory. But to then conclude that it is a mere instrument for a higher form of monastic life is a logical leap that I find unwarranted. It seems to me that Benedict lays himself open to this kind of misinterpretation. Yet the Bible certainly regards Christian community as a primary value, and the remainder of the Holy Rule does the same.

Beyond Asceticism

As I have pointed out, the first part of Benedict's Rule is very much under the thrall and influence of the Rule of the Master. Not only does that tend to give it an individual, vertical cast, but it also puts a great deal of emphasis on asceticism. I use the word "asceticism" here not so much to connote penance but rather struggle. The Greek term *askesis* means exactly that: hard striving, strenuous labor. It can be used to refer to athletic training or to spiritual effort, but the key idea is struggle. When we read over the Prologue to the Rule of Benedict from this angle, it is plain that this is the keynote: monastic life is a hard, uphill battle, a great effort. If we are ready to make that effort, we are welcome to take on the habit; if not, we can freely depart.

But I think it is important, even crucial, to point out that this is not the only message of the Prologue. At the very end of that long chapter, in verses 47-49, we read as follows:

> In a given case we may have to arrange things a bit strictly to correct vice or preserve charity. When that happens, do not immediately take fright and flee the path of salvation, which can only be narrow at its outset. But as we progress in the monastic life and in faith, our hearts will swell with the unspeakable sweetness of love, enabling us to race along the way of God's commandments.

Before we exegete this passage, we must note its structural significance, namely, it is an addition of Benedict to the text of the Rule of the Master. Throughout most of the Prologue, Benedict is faithfully copying the Prologue of the Master, but at verses 45-50, he breaks off and inserts his own conclusion. In my opinion, this is very significant. Why has he done this? He must have thought he had to finally break into the Master's long Prologue and add his own conclusion.

I think the reason for this becomes clear enough when we note the contents. As we said, the message of the Master's Prologue is basically ascesis: You have been drifting through life, you have been asleep, and so forth. If you want to be a monk, you have to rise up and take up the hard effort of a disciplined and serious life. Surely Benedict agrees with it or he would have not quoted the Master for forty verses! But he seems to think that he must add something, and that something is very important.

What does he add? To put it in a nutshell, he adds love. "Our hearts will swell with the unspeakable sweetness of love." Apparently he feels he must interject this promise, and he does it in a most memorable manner. He presents the monastic life not just as a hard, uphill struggle, but also as a race. And this is not just an ordinary race. In a typical, physical race, the further we run, the more tired we get, until we finally run out of steam. But Benedict seems to think that the monastic life, and indeed the spiritual life, is different. If we live it right, we will grow stronger as we go, not weaker. This is a special kind of strength; this is vigor that comes from joy. "Our hearts will swell with the unspeakable sweetness of love" (RB Prol.49).

In order to appreciate the full power of this teaching, it is important to put it in context. If we look again at the Rule of the Master we can see what Benedict has done. The Master ends like Benedict with this sentence: "We will participate in the passion of Christ through patience so as to deserve to be companions in his kingdom. Amen" (Prol.50). But since the Master says nothing about the joyful running and the swelling heart, it looks very much as if the Master thinks the essence of the monastic life is suffering. Since he also says that this patient suffering will lead us to the Kingdom of God, we may feel that he is on the right track.

But apparently Benedict thinks it is not exactly the right track. He does not seem willing to agree that the core meaning of the monastic life is suffering, even patient suffering. Which is to say that ascesis is not the essence of the spiritual life. Granted, all genuine monasticism contains an element of ascetic struggle, but it is important to remember that that struggle, that effort, is secondary. It is a means to the end, but the end is not struggle; the end is joy.

It is true that the Master does understand this progression, but in a different way than Benedict. In fact, the two authors have a different eschatology. For the Master, the monastic life is one long battle, but the reward is great. Yet the reward is not in this world; it is in heaven. In two places (RM 3.78-94 and 10.92-122), the Master breaks out into long, quite ecstatic, descriptions of heaven. For him, heaven will be a cornucopia of delights, almost a kind of sensual heaven. For his part, Benedict quietly drops these provocative, but also somewhat infantile, passages. For Benedict, heaven starts now, not hereafter.

This is the basic significance of his talk about joy in verse 49 of the Prologue. For the monk, spiritual joy is not something completely deferred as it seems to be for the Master. For Benedict, the monastic life, if it is what it is meant to be, should be one of joy and delight. It is not primarily grim struggle. As Benedict points out, it can sometimes feel like an uphill climb. But that is a false impression that we should not succumb to. Actually, a moment's reflection will convince us that this is so.

In many aspects of life, we might even say *all* worthwhile human endeavors, the beginnings will be hard. Why this is true will be obvious in certain endeavors. When I strive to learn a craft or a skill, things usually do not immediately fall into place. No, I must struggle through the learning process. The piano player must learn the scales and then practice, practice, practice. Our muscles and reflexes need to be trained, and the training will often be painful. But in many cases, there is a breakthrough. At some point, things become less of a struggle and more of a joy. At some point, I can make music without much struggle. I then have *joy* in music.

In technical theological terms, this means that Benedict believes in *realized eschatology*. Unlike the Master, that is, unlike his literary prototype, he thinks that the ordinary monk can, if he perseveres in the monastic program, actually hope to eventually find it a joy and a blessing. If it does not become that, then there is real question about vocation. The monk who finds the life a continual penance is probably in the wrong game.

Recalling the Main Theme

At this point, and before we complete this section, we might recall the main theme or themes of our work here. Our title is *Benedict Backwards*, and we pointed out that this means that we will give greater emphasis to the end of his Rule than to the beginning. We do this because we believe that Benedict himself begins his Rule somewhat "captive" to an earlier writer, namely, the Master. We said that only gradually does Benedict leave off copying, therefore finding his own voice, his own stride, as it were. This is generally true as regards the element of community and interpersonal relations.

Yet it is not an iron rule that has no exceptions. In this essay, we have been discussing the remarkable assertion of Professor Albrecht Diem that Benedict is less focused on community than another early rule, namely, *Regula Cuiusdam*. In coping with this assertion, which I cannot accept, I have had to admit that there are aspects of Benedict's Rule that can leave the wrong impression. As Diem notes, the element of love is not as prominent as humility, obedience, and silence. But we pointed out that this is because those are the primary values of the Master. Once Benedict achieves some separation from the RM, love will take its proper place, and it will finally predominate over humility and obedience.

But beyond that, Benedict's dependence on the Master in the first pages of his Rule also has the effect of stressing the individual more than the community. There is not much reference to the common life in the first seven chapters of RB, although it is not completely absent. Despite the rather confusing comparisons in RB 1, the overall thrust of RB is not to give anchoritism more importance than cenobitism. As we noted, it never mentions hermits again after RB 1. The Holy Rule is for cenobites, not anchorites.

We then discussed Benedict's special closing to his Prologue. Even though this may seem to depart a bit from our overall themes, I don't think it does. As we concluded, verses 47-49 in the Prologue focus on the joyful aspect of monastic existence. It is my conviction that this remarkable assertion, which comes very early in the Rule, is completely in harmony with Benedict's general focus on Christian community life. Of course, spiritual joy is essential to any form of Christian life, including the solitary form. But I would contend that joy has special relevance in community life.

A lifetime of lived experience in Benedictine community convinces me that joy is a crucial component of life together. We sometimes read in ancient spiritual authors, such as St. John Climacus, of monasteries where sorrow and weeping were the norm. Indeed, one Egyptian monastery was named *metanoia*, "penitence." No doubt some of those people had much to repent from their past lives. But ordinary, healthy cenobites, especially in our times of general psychic stress, have a great need of joy in the Lord. When we have that, we are a gift to each other, and such joy radiates to the group. Thank God for the joyful, cheerful monks among us!

Chapter 6

Hate Self-Will!

One of the sufferings awaiting the person who writes something down, and especially one who publishes it, is to catch yourself having uttered nonsense. Specifically, in my translation of the Rule of Benedict (1996) I wrote, "Hate your own will" (RB 4.60). How could I have written such a thing? How could Benedict have written such a thing? In this essay I will try to show (1) that Benedict actually did *not* write such a thing, and (2) it is not so difficult to make mistakes when translating the Latin terms involved here.

First of all, the Latin words are *voluntatem propriam*. Now, that phrase is ambiguous, since it can mean "your own will" or "self-will." Although we do not use it much anymore, "self-will" often has a pejorative meaning. It refers to the insistence that my will and no other is what counts, and that is what I will follow. It is associated with stubbornness, hubris, and downright arrogance. Nobody enjoys an encounter with a truly self-willed person, and it is especially excoriated by the legislators of cenobitic monasticism.

On the other hand, "my will" or "your own will" can hardly be an evil or something to be eliminated. The will is an essential component of the human personality, and to denigrate it or seek to eradicate it is a terrible perversion. This can be seen in the infamous process called "brainwashing," in which one person uses devious psychological methods to weaken or even erase the willpower of another person. The fact that this infamous process has been used on a mass scale in modern times, actually throughout history, does not in any way excuse it.

The Rule of the Master

It should be no surprise that the issue of the human will is an important one in ancient monastic literature. For example, the now-famous Rule of the Master seems almost obsessed with the matter, which is obvious from the sheer amount of space devoted to it. In a paper I published in Spain (*Studia Monastica*, 2000, pp. 319–46), I presented a detailed analysis of all of the major passages in the RM that develop this topic. In this essay I will not repeat that lengthy and intricate data; rather, I will try to synthesize it into a comprehensive package.

We begin with the plain fact that the Master has a very negative idea of the human will. In his view, to put it very bluntly, whatever we will is evil. He never says that the will itself is evil, or, to use Lutheran language, utterly perverted, but it is not hard to draw that conclusion from much that he does say about our willing. At times he tones down this extremely harsh viewpoint by saying that self-will is whatever is consciously done *against* the will of God (RM ThP.30). But all too often he does not qualify it in that fashion, leaving us with the bitter notion that we cannot will the good.

It should be noted that there is another qualification at work here that does take some of the edge off of the Master's attack on the human will. He often speaks of our willing as "desire," (*desiderium*), and it is usually obvious that he is referring to our physical drives. Now the curious thing is that the Latin for these urges is *voluptas*, and the reader does not have to be too learned or acute to see how close this is to *voluntas* (will). The difference is merely one letter, but the difference in meaning is very much greater. My will and my urges are by no means the same thing. Indeed, any mature person knows that a successful life involves precisely the control of the urges by the will.

In our own time, not everybody is ready to agree that physical desires are bad or even dangerous. In fact, the Catholic Church, which has a bad reputation for sexual prudery, nowhere teaches that all physical desire is problematic. It does appear, however, that the Master does indeed think along those lines. For example, in exegeting John 6:38, "I came not to do my own will but the will of the one who sent me," the Master explains that Jesus here gives us an example "so that the free will *of the flesh* will be suppressed in us" (RM ThP.34). This is by no means an isolated saying; the Master says things like this so often that one can easily conclude that when he talks about the will, he is really talking about concupiscence.

How, then, can we overcome this great weakness in ourselves? According to the Master, the only adequate solution is that the will of God must *replace* our will! This radical, if breathtaking, solution seems to satisfy the Master's amazingly simpleminded anthropology. It does not seem to occur to him that such a replacement would completely eliminate human freedom. It would also put an end to human responsibility. It would seem to solve the problem of evil, but it would also undo the basic elements of God's creation of the human species.

Admittedly, there are biblical texts that can be interpreted in this manner. For example, Jesus in the Garden of Gethsemane says to God, "Not my will but thine be done" (Matt 26:39). At first the Master comes up with a respectable interpretation of this admittedly hard verse. He says that Jesus is here repudiating his own *actus vitae*, which could be translated as "will to live." But after mulling this for a few more verses, the Master comes to another, astonishing conclusion: "See, therefore, that whatever we choose by our will is patently unjust, and whatever is justly imposed on us by the one who has command over us is accounted to our credit." In my judgment, this is a good example of exegesis gone haywire—and basically gone mad. It is a repudiation of the human will that is so thoroughgoing as to call into question all human goodness.

Unfortunately, that may not be too far from the Master's overall assessment of the average person. When discussing the cenobites in RM 1.87, he refers to them as "all who still have folly as their mother," a reference to the theme of wisdom and folly in the Hebrew Wisdom Literature. Since this is the way the Master describes the monastic candidates, it seems that he has an abysmally low estimate of the human race. So what hope is there for us? Again, to replace our own silly will with that of another, namely, someone who can show us the will of God. For a cenobitic monk, that someone is the abbot.

But can we be sure that the abbot will communicate God's will to us? According to the Master, yes, we can. In fact, he is not afraid to make the following statement: "This is so because whether for good or for ill, what happens among the sheep is the responsibility of the shepherd, and he who gave orders is the one who will have to render an account when inquiry is made at the judgment, not he who carried out the orders, good or bad" (RM 7.55-56). Anyone who detects a whiff of the self-defense made at Nuremberg by the Nazi war criminals can be excused. In saying this, the Master has certainly departed from basic Catholic moral teaching. We are never excused from judging the acts we are asked to perform.

The Master also does not hesitate to draw various pernicious corollaries from these principles. One of them has to do with the concept of thwarting, that is, not letting people do what they want to do. Now of course this is a basic principle in all human discipline, for obvious reasons. We do not let babies put harmful things in their mouths. But when it comes to adults, the plot thickens because adults are by definition free and, by and large, do what they please. They cannot be allowed to do harmful things to others, but it is basically not a healthy thing to thwart people from their wishes. That, however, does not stop the Master from deliberately instituting a program of monastic formation that is based entirely on making people do what they do not want to do and preventing them from doing what they want. This tough philosophy is enunciated in RM 90.60-62 and *passim*:

> So when someone, drawing near the fear of God, desires to live the monastic life and wants to be a disciple, let his future master in the Lord's name explain to him, as we have said above, that whatever he at any time tries to get by his own will's desire may, he should know, be refused him, and whatever he does not want may, let him hear, be imposed on him.

This same approach to monastic formation is also espoused by John Cassian (Conf 9.14; 18.7) who is one of the Master's mentors. Cassian cheerfully recommends the creation of clever schemes meant to frustrate the novice. Why? Because he must learn to distrust his own will. Those, like the writer of these lines, who passed through cenobitic formation fifty years ago probably can recognize the mentality and the methods. Lurking behind such thinking is the theme of the "monk as martyr," which the Master explicitly expounds in RM 7.59. But at this point we have said enough about the Master's theory of self-will and will. It is time to turn to Saint Benedict.

The Rule of Benedict

The first thing to note about Benedict's discussion of self-will is that it is not as important for him as it is for the Master. In terms of statistics, Benedict uses the term *voluntas* one-fifth as often as does the Master. Since the overall text of the RM is about three times longer than that of RB, this suggests that the theme is of less significance for Benedict. This kind of statistical argument should not be overemphasized, but it does point in a certain direction. Self-will is not a huge concern for Benedict. To put this argument another way, of the five principal passages where the Master discusses this subject, Benedict reproduces only two.

In terms of our general claim in these pages that Benedict follows the Master most closely in the first seven chapters of his Rule, this should be seen as an exception, but a significant exception. As a matter of fact, Benedict omits large chunks of the Master, even in the part where he is most dependent. It is not so easy to evaluate these omissions since it is impossible to prove a negative. Why did the dog not bark? Still, we can say that Benedict has chosen to skip over precisely some of the most problematic statements of the Master concerning self-will. As we have seen, some of the Master's ideas are more helpful than others in this matter. In my view, Benedict has managed to avoid the worst ones! That said, let us examine the three passages of Benedict on this subject. First, we have a statement that occurs in RB 5 on obedience:

> Therefore they seize on the narrow way, of which the Lord says: "The route that leads to life is narrow." That is why they do not wish to live by their own lights, obeying their own desires and wants. Rather, they prefer to walk according to the judgment and command of another, living in cenobitic community with an abbot over them. (RB 5.11-13)

When I first dipped my toe into RB studies, and began reading Adalbert de Vogüé's commentaries, I ran across his interpretation of this text, and it shocked me. According to him, Benedict here teaches that a cenobitic monk, when he makes his vow of obedience, thereby abandons his own judgment. My understanding of moral theology is that one of the things we can never, ever abandon is our own conscience. But in this passage, or at least in de Vogüé's interpretation of it, this is exactly what we are being asked to do. Since I was soon to go to Rome to study with the French savant, I mentally filed this question for a later date. When I asked him in person, I expected de Vogüé to nuance his remarks, but he did not back down an inch! At that time, I could not understand why he thought he had to absolutize a text like this.

Certainly, Benedict's text as it stands is difficult. Some of the problem is no doubt linguistic. For example, a key word, judgment (*arbitrium*), has a different flavor in Latin than it does in English. None of the meanings given in the *Oxford Latin Dictionary* are negative, but in English to be "arbitrary" is not a compliment. It means that one tends to make snap decisions more or less on a whim. It is the opposite of *discernment*, which implies careful consideration of a problem. Another word to be noted is *voluptatibus*. Here again, as with the Master (whom Benedict is quoting word for word), this is a rather surprising term. But remember that *voluptas* and *voluntas* are spelled almost identically. At the very least, there is a confusion here in what is really being discussed. Considered judgments or physical urges?

To come back to de Vogüé, who would surely still stand his ground against me, I have come to the conclusion that it was his very method that caused him to make such stunning interpretations. For him, one can understand Benedict only against the *full background* of the Master's doctrine. Since we have already laid out that doctrine in some detail, we can say that the Master really believed that the obedient monk no longer operates by his own judgment at all. He has completely given himself over to the "judgment of another." He simply follows what he has been told; he does not subject it to his own evaluation, and he certainly does not go against it in his actions.

As for me, I fully understand that the obedient monk does not normally second-guess the teachings or the orders of the abbot. He knows that he can trust the wisdom of the community in electing this particular man. He might not find all his ideas convincing, but he knows that he will probably not go wrong in following him. Note, however, that word "probably." There still does exist the possibility that the abbot is wrong. The Master, of course, cannot accept this, and neither could de Vogüé. But a cursory reading of RB 2 shows that Benedict does not seem to have any trouble imagining abbatial confusion or even bad will. As for the monk, he retains the right and duty of judging such teaching, and it is still his decision whether or not to live by it. Benedict never goes so far as to say, as the Master does, that whatever we do under obedience is therefore, *ipso facto*, good (RM 7.53-56).

Lest I be misunderstood in this matter, let me repeat that I think that Adalbert de Vogüé, who was probably the greatest modern expert on the Rule of Benedict, nevertheless was seriously misguided in his use of the Rule of the Master to interpret RB. In a sense, this is understandable since de Vogüé was also the greatest expert (no doubt, of all time) on the Rule of the Master. But unfortunately that Rule is full of dubious, and sometimes blatant, errors. To "fill out" Benedict's material with the RM, as de Vogüé always does, is often a dangerous procedure. It seems to me that this has led de Vogüé seriously astray on a question like self-will. But let us move on to another passage of Benedict, namely, his teaching on the importance of humility versus self-will. Here is a capital text for our discussion (RB 7.19-25):

> As for self-will, we are forbidden to carry it out, for Scripture says to us: "Beware of your own desires" (Sir 18:30). And so we ask God in prayer that his will be accomplished in us. Thus it is with good reason that we learn to steer clear of our own will, for we dread the warning of Holy Scripture: "There are paths that seem straight to us, but ultimately they plunge into the depths of hell" (Prov 16:25). . . . We should be convinced that our lower inclinations are well known to God, for the Prophet says to God: "All my desire is before you" (Ps 37:10). Thus it is imperative that we beware of evil desire, for death lurks near the gateway of pleasure. That is why Scripture commands: "Do not pursue your lusts" (Sir 18:30).

I have quoted this passage at length because it shows that Benedict thinks along the same lines as the Master on some of these matters. After all, he is quoting the Master verbatim in this whole section. In general, he can do this without damage, because this passage does not contain any of the Master's erroneous ideas.

The passage starts out with a stark statement of the main point: we are not permitted to carry out self-will. But when we think about that condemnation, we still have to ask what self-will is. If it refers to what we originally presented as real, morally reprehensible self-will, namely, to deliberately reject the true will of God in favor of our own preference, then there is no problem: Reject self-will! We will never go wrong not carrying it out.

The problem, as I see it, however, is that all too often a text like this slides over into something quite different. For example, when I was a novice it often seemed to me that we were being subjected to a system of *thwarting*. That is to say, whatever we wanted, that was what we could not have. Of course, this kind of pedagogical brutality was never explicitly stated, but the implication was clear enough: what you want is beside the point; we will tell you what to want. I remember that I, at least, quickly learned that the best way to cope with such a system was to never reveal what I really wanted. That way I saved myself a lot of trouble and frustration.

The difficulty here, however, is the implication that whatever I want is bad and wrong. But surely that is not true: our wills are not totally corrupted! Furthermore, this kind of thwarting can have the long-term effect of suppression where I finally do not really *know* what I want. Now many people in our society complain of this: they don't know what they really want, and that is regarded as an affliction and a barrier to true maturation and fulfillment. Why should the monastic system of formation promote such nonsense? Should not our formation really be about helping people come to know what they really, truly want?

Little did we realize in those days, before any of us knew about the Rule of the Master, that this was exactly what that confused teacher proposed as the ideal of monastic formation: thwarting!

> To test him, let difficulties be made, and to ascertain his obedience let him be told in advance about things contrary and repugnant to his will. . . . To say "I want this and I reject that, I like this and I hate that," is allowed to no one in the monastery, so that self-will be not chosen and indulged. And let him know that whoever wishes to live the religious life perfectly in the monastery will all the more not be permitted what he desires according to his own will. (RM 90.3-6)

We should note right away that this is not a text that Benedict reproduces! In fact, he has completely ignored RM 90 on formation.

Some scholars say that it is no wonder Benedict ignored it since it had not been written in his time. That is a technical question that cannot be gone into. But I would add that John Cassian sometimes suggests this kind of thwarting as good monastic discipline.

In response, let me tell a little story on myself. When I was a fairly young monk, I went to the abbot and said to him: "I am worried about myself." When he asked why, I answered, "Because you seem to let me do whatever I want." The abbot did not respond immediately, but eventually he said: "As I see it, the real question is *do you want what you ought to want?*" After fifty years (and more) as monk, I cannot think of a wiser remark by a monastic authority.

A third passage where Benedict discusses the will of the monk and the need to transcend it lies in RB 33. This is a rather radical little treatise in which Benedict insists that all personal possessions be "rooted out" from the cenobite. To show that he means this literally, he even gives us a sort of checklist: "no book, no writing tablets, no stylus—nothing whatsoever" (33.3). Now a moment's consideration will tell us that this cannot be meant absolutely, since monks, like everybody else, must at least *use* the goods of the world: they must eat and wear clothes. Besides that, Benedict provides us with something of a rationale for the practice of personal dispossession.

In RB 33.4 he enunciates what some scholars consider the central core of the chapter: "That is because they have neither their bodies nor their own wills at their own disposal." First, we might note that our target phrase turns up here again: *in propria voluntate*. My own translation of these words is as follows: "at their own disposal." De Vogüé and Lentini both think that Benedict probably meant to write *potestate* here, that is, "power," which is a better word-choice here than *voluntate*, which normally means "will." At any rate, we certainly have here one of those instances where *propria voluntas* does not and cannot mean "self-will," which would make no sense in this context. As always, in rendering these words we have to judge each case on its own merits.

Next, we have to take into account the fact that the term "bodies," which is quite clear, *corpora sua*, can hardly be taken literally. There is no warrant in Catholic moral thinking for one person, even an abbot, having the body of another person, even a monk, at his disposal. One of the inalienable human rights is to dispose of one's own body, for good or ill. Even Benedict's radical claims for dispossession in cenobites cannot supersede this human right. Then what does "bodies" mean here? Taken together with "wills" (*voluntates*), it must refer to the whole person. The two together could be rendered as "selves," as that which the cenobite freely "donates" to the community in the person of the abbot.

The great Basilian scholar Jean Gribomont thought that the probable background for this verse is to be found in the writings of St. Basil of Cappadoccia. In Latin Rule 29 he says: "Since Christ gave his life for us, how can we consider our own that which is much less personal (i.e., chattels) than our life?" In another of his Rules (106), Basil directly connects the *kenosis* (self-effacement) of Christ with monastic dispossession. In both RB 33 and for Basil, the argument is *a fortiori*: from the lesser (material possessions) to the greater (our whole self).

Whether Benedict had these texts of Basil in the back of his mind when he wrote RB 33, I do not know, but I have to say that he was also greatly influenced by another Christian monastic master, namely, John Cassian. (There is no parallel chapter to RB 33 in the Rule of the Master). In his *Institutes* 7, Cassian has a fascinating discussion of the vice of avarice. Among other things, he feels that avarice is a vice that is particularly contagious, in the sense that it tends to spread like wildfire. In fact, Cassian compares it to noxious weeds that must be entirely rooted out if they are not to dominate the whole field. This is the basis for his idea that they must be "rooted out," a strong image that Benedict also takes up. Actually, Benedict uses it at the beginning and the end of RB 33, which probably signals that the problem of avarice was in his mind for the whole chapter.

At any rate, RB 33 is an example of how Benedict is quite capable of discussing the human will and the need to control it without falling back on any of the dubious ideas of the Rule of the Master in this regard. I think it is especially important in matters like this that the interpreter *not* assume that Benedict thinks just like the Master. He makes extensive use of the RM where it suits his purposes, but he is not at all beholden to it where it does not.

Chapter 7

Simplicity

Some years ago I was asked to address a meeting of Quakers and Benedictines, and the first subject of common interest that leaped to my mind was simplicity. Actually, that was a favorite *Shaker* theme, but nonetheless I pursued it. But when I tried to do a word-study of it in the Rule of Benedict, I did not come up with much; there are only four instances of *simplicitas* and three of them are decidedly banal. Yet when I pressed my research further, I found that this theme is indeed a monastic one.

For example, Jean Leclercq chose to include it in his book, *Studies on the Monastic Vocabulary of the Middle Ages* (1961), where he said: "Simplicity is characteristic of a monk; one could say that it is the monastic virtue par excellence." So even if the term "simple" does not turn up very often in the RB, we can expect that the idea, the thing, is there when we look hard. Indeed, the very word "monk" is based on a Greek word (*monos*) that refers to simplicity. Mark Sheridan wrote a rich essay on this term in *RB 1980* (pp. 301–21) in which he showed that the monk must be integrated and focused on one point: God.

Physical Simplicity: Frugality

Before we explore the moral and spiritual depths of simplicity, we should look at the physical aspects of the idea. One of those dimensions is what we might call frugality, namely, an aversion to wastefulness. In fact, Saint Benedict emphasizes this virtue in his monks, and especially in the cellarer. Since that monastic official has the special duty of managing the community property, it is not surprising that Benedict would demand that he or she not squander those goods. In fact, his brilliant chapter on the cellarer twice issues a warning against wastefulness (*non prodigus*). Yet it would not be correct to conclude that this is Benedict's *key* value, since he also wants the cellarer to not be stingy.

I am somewhat sensitive to the need for proper balance in these matters since as a child I suffered from the ministrations of a baby-sitter who was fanatically stingy. She used to buy *unlabeled* canned goods because they were cheaper, but of course we never knew what was in those cans. She eventually ruined herself in old age when she used to unscrew the lightbulbs in the house to save electricity. But when this causes people to fall down dark stairwells such frugality obviously becomes absurd.

Benedict himself sometimes risks falling into the same kind of senseless opposition to material things. In his chapter 33, "Whether Monks Should Consider Anything Their Own," he begins: "This vice in particular must be torn up by the roots, that anyone should presume to give or receive anything without the abbot's permission, or consider anything personal property." Now, of course, cenobitic monks do hold all things in common, so personal greed can be a problem. But on the other hand, to give the impression that monks can live at all without *using* material possessions is ridiculous.

Actually, Benedict's chapter 33 is based on *Institutes* 7 of John Cassian, concerning *avarice*. In that very insightful discussion, Cassian points out that avarice has the unfortunate effect of burgeoning in a person: greedy people tend to become more and more greedy, especially for money. Furthermore, he claims that this is a vice that, like some noxious weeds, must be totally eradicated. Half measures will not do since it always grows back. Benedict used Cassian's ideas to good effect, but unfortunately they also give RB 33 a somewhat fanatical effect. In fact, avarice is *not* the worst Christian vice. Pride is.

At any rate, Benedict redeems himself in the very next chapter when he discusses monastic frugality or dispossession from another angle. In RB 34, he asks whether all monks need exactly the same things from the community. This little chapter, which is based on the Bible and not Stoic philosophy as with Cassian, says that people should get what they need; only then will there be peace in the monastery (see 1 Cor 12:26). But since different people have different needs, that means that there really cannot be equal distribution. Those who need more should receive more; those who need less should get less—and not grumble.

Simple as this sounds, it is in fact profoundly countercultural, at least in our society. We live in a materialist, consumerist culture that is tied to industrial production and capitalist growth. We are virtually *taught* to want more and use more. To keep the factories humming and the goods flying off the shelves at Walmart, we need to keep spending. The modern consumerist "saint" is the person who needs and demands more, not less. Still, we should remember that material goods as such are never evil. The New Testament basis for frugality is the need to serve others, to give them what they need. That is why RB 34 is a good corrective to RB 33.

Moral Simplicity: Integrity

In discussing frugality, we have already seen that it has some complex dimensions. The basic reason for this lies in the very nature of the human person. To put it simply, we are not simple. We are a composite of the physical and the mental or spiritual, which is a fact that everyone with any self-awareness knows perfectly well. As such, this "duality" has its own problems and its glories. For example, we humans have it in us to be profoundly devious, hiding our real feelings and intentions from the onlooker. With us, the outside is by no means the same as the inside, or at least it can be so. By and large, moralists frown on this unfortunate human split, urging us to avoid hypocrisy. In this, Saint Benedict is no different.

In fact, two of Benedict's seventy-four aphorisms in his chapter 4, titled "Instruments of Good Works," preach candor against hypocrisy. RB 4.28 reads: "Speak the truth both in your heart and with your mouth." Of course, strictly speaking the heart does not speak; only the mouth does. But Benedict here seems to be guarding against mental reservations. At least that is one way of reading the verse. Certainly, he is not demanding that we blurt out everything that comes into our heads. But on the other hand, he does not seem to have much use for the complicated, crafty person who often means something other than what he actually says. Benedict does not want devious monks.

Another version of the same teaching on integrity can be seen in RB 4.62: "Do not wish to be called holy before you really are; first be holy and then the term will be truer in your case." In this verse, Benedict seems to risk forfeiting his status as an Italian! Why? Because one of the great Italian values is *la bella figura*, in colloquial American, "Lookin' good." This may be the root of the famous Italian penchant for "style," good-looking clothes, good-looking cars, and so on. *La bella figura* also has produced one of the most beautiful countries in the world in terms of art and architecture.

But *la bella figura* is by no means a unilaterally helpful attitude toward life. In plain language, looking good is not the same as being good. There is a strange, even disastrous, passage in the Rule of the Master (RM 92) where the monk is counselled to look good (that is, humble, obedient, and so on) in front of the abbot. Why? So he will be chosen by the abbot as his successor! In other words, the monks are urged to put up a good front for the boss. In the face of such blatant hypocrisy, Benedict no doubt threw up his hands. At any rate, he makes no mention whatsoever of this chapter of RM. He wants the monks to choose as abbot the wisest and best man for the job, even if he is the youngest member.

Certainly, Benedict wants integrity from his abbot. In RB 2.11-12, he says: "Furthermore, when someone accepts the title of abbot, he should direct his disciples by a twofold teaching. That means he should demonstrate everything that is good and holy by his deeds more than by his words. He should teach gifted disciples by words, but he will have to personally model the divine precepts for those who are recalcitrant or naïve." This is a demanding job! It is not enough for the abbot to have a beautiful *doctrina*. Unlike a college professor, he does not go home at night; he is a live-in teacher whom the disciples can and do observe from morning to night. If they think, "He can talk the talk, but he can't walk the walk," this undermines his monastic authority.

Many years ago the abbot of my monastery created a minor sensation in the community by his appointment of a new master of clerics. The man in question was a surprising choice, since he was the least "observant" monk in the monastery! That is to say, he did not, and perhaps could not, live by the ordinary rules. When he gave his inaugural conference to the junior monks, they were all anxious to hear what on earth he would say. He said, in a soft, quivering voice: "Do what I say, not what I do!" End of conference.

Another saying of Benedict urging candid simplicity occurs in the twelfth step of humility: "The twelfth step of humility is achieved when a monk's humility is not only in his heart but apparent in his very body to those who see him." The argument here is the reverse of what we usually hear in regard to integrity. Instead of being warned against inner hypocrisy, we are now told that we need to exhibit externally what we believe internally. This is not an easy teaching for a certain modern mentality (like the author's!), which distrusts any blatant display of virtue or holiness. Yet are we not supposed to be a light to the world?

The thoughtful reader may by this time be wondering when this essay will deal with the negative connotations of simplicity. After all, we also use this term to refer to excessively simpleminded persons. "Simpleton" is not a compliment. Obviously, monasticism is not meant to promote or nurture simplemindedness! There is no virtue in ignorance as such. Because of certain remarks by St. Athanasius in his famous *Life of Antony*, we used to extoll the Father of Monks because he had no books and read no books. Yet, recent studies have shown, thank God, that in fact Antony was familiar with the sophisticated theology of Alexandria.

There is such a thing as *second simplicity*. This evocative concept is employed by Raimon Panikkar (*Blessed Simplicity*, 1982, pp. 35–39) to describe the condition of the monk or any spiritual seeker who has passed beyond the renunciation of things to a further state. At this point, says the Indian savant, a person is able to appreciate all things, no matter how multiple, but as a means of access to the oneness or unicity of God. We will pick this theme up again in our last section.

Moral Simplicity: Focus

Another form of moral simplicity may be termed *focus*. The word here refers to aiming at a target or object. But more precisely, it means to aim at *one* target, and the right target. As a general principle, this idea is easy to appreciate: unless we are aimed in the right direction, we are liable, nay, we are *sure* to go badly astray. Where does this concept turn up in the Rule of Benedict?

I think that it achieves remarkable prominence in the penultimate chapter, namely, RB 72 "The Good Zeal That Monks Ought to Have." This intriguing title contains a word that is not much used in ordinary English discourse but that has great significance: zeal. It is a term that occurs in much the same form in both Greek and Latin, and which refers to great energy or enthusiasm for something. A famous biblical quote is "Zeal for your house has consumed me" (Ps 69:9, my translation). The point here is that the Psalmist loves to come and pray in the temple.

But zeal in itself, although it is full of dynamic power, is also ambivalent. That is to say that it can go in any direction. Saint Benedict understands this very well as he demonstrates in the beginning of RB 72: "Just as there is an evil and bitter zeal that separates one from God and leads to hell, so too there is a good zeal that separates one from evil and leads to God and eternal life." So the author lets us know that he is dealing here with a fairly dangerous element. This is a "hot-button issue," to use current parlance. Yet although Benedict is fully aware that he is touching on something fairly risky, he is not afraid to push ahead with it.

And what is "it"? Love! Love is the good zeal that monks ought to have, love for God and for one another. But we must also remember that there is an underside to love, namely, hatred. If zeal is not aimed in the right direction as love, it is likely to land on some unfortunate targets. Someone might say, "Well, since that is the case, would it be better to have *no* zeal? That way, we will at least avoid going way off the track." Unfortunately, no zeal is also a perfect formula for indifference and even spiritual death. No, there is no real possibility of avoiding the issue of properly aiming our zeal—the assumption here is that we all *do have innate zeal for the good and for God.*

In the present world situation, when this essay is being written (2015), we seem to have a good deal of extremely bad religious zeal boiling up around us. Since the partisans of ISIS and Al-Qaeda and the Taliban all claim to be motivated with zeal for Allah, we have to take them at their word. But we also cannot help but notice that their zeal has lead them to unspeakable deeds of violence and inhumanity. To use Benedict's terminology, this is a classic example of bad zeal. But we also should notice that such people say that their ultimate target is the godless West, in other words, people of *no zeal*.

A second possible instance of moral simplicity as intensive focus might be seen in Benedict's instructions regarding the admittance of candidates into his monastery. RB 58.7 reads: "One must note whether he really seeks God, and whether he is serious about the Work of God, obedience, and hardships." A cursory reading of this verse indicates that the key idea lies in the seeking of God; the remainder of the considerations, namely, the Work of God, obedience, and hardships, should be understood as aspects of the central concern, that is, the seeking of God. In this regard, we may say that the adverb in the sentence is crucial: "Whether he *really* seeks God."

The Latin original for *really* in this sentence is *revera*, which could also be translated "truly," honestly," and so on. Actually, it is an intrinsically banal expression that can function as a blank that is then filled in with our ideas about what the novice *really* should be after. A close examination of the Latin does not help much: *re vera* just means "true thing" or "real thing." But at least it makes clear that the great thing here, the real point at issue, is again *focus*. What is the novice really after? What is she or he aiming for? The obvious answer is "God," but that still leaves a great deal unanswered.

It seems to me that even though Benedict's language here is fairly vague, it is nevertheless very helpful. For it lets us know that the real purpose of the novitiate is to find out why I have come to the monastery. Somebody once said that about college, and I think it could be extended to life itself: the great project in college is to figure out why I am in college. When it comes to the joining a monastery, we have to say that there are many possible reasons and many of them are bad. Perhaps almost all of them are bad—except the right one! But, as we said above, we humans are not simple creatures; we are complicated, and we might even say that we are largely opaque to ourselves. We often do not know why we do what we do. So it is no disgrace to come to the monastery for the wrong reasons. Of course, that discovery may be a legitimate reason to leave, but I think Benedict is telling us here that the key task of the novice master is to help the novice sort out her motivations, and if possible, settle on the right one.

This is not to imply that it is an easy thing to discover if I "really, truly, seek God." Indeed, the matter will usually be approached somewhat indirectly. For example, in his monthly conference with a novice, a certain master asked: "Well, are you happy?" It seems like an obvious question, but it shocked the novice! He blurted out that he did not know he was supposed to be happy; in fact, since he had come to the monastery partly to atone for his sins, he assumed he probably should not be overly happy. Being happy and seeking God are not exactly the same thing, but still, they must be pretty closely connected. There are many other questions that broach the same basic issue: is this what God wants of me?

Spiritual Simplicity: Oneness with God

We have not yet arrived at the deepest level of our inquiry, which must be somewhat metaphysical. That term is not much seen today in spiritual writing, and it probably scares the wits out of most people. As for Benedict, it is probably true to say that there is not a single purely metaphysical discussion in his Rule. He is a practical man, which does not mean he is not subtle. But, unlike the Rule of the Master, he is not given to abstract, theoretical discussions. Before we look for some element of spiritual simplicity in the Rule, we should try to explain what it means here.

The basic, metaphysical truth about God, at least for our purposes here, is that he is one. This is the great claim of monotheism, but what does it mean? It can mean many things, but at the most elementary level it means that God has no parts. This also means that God is simple, in the Latin sense of *simplex*, one-piece. For the ancient philosophers, this was to say a great deal about God, for that which has no parts cannot deteriorate. Therefore, God is eternal and unchangeable. This kind of talk is perhaps less impressive to the modern mentality, which loves change. But in strictly metaphysical terms, it is doing God no favor to say he can change. God is one.

There are endless elaborations on such a claim. Saint Augustine, for example, thought that God's simplicity largely means that he cannot lose his attributes. Put another way, God not only *has* certain qualities; he *is* certain qualities. To say John is honest does not mean that he cannot cease to be honest, or that he is not perhaps partly dishonest. But to say that God is honest or true means that God's truth does not come and go. Truth is part of the very definition of God. He cannot not be true. Rather than prolong such lucubrations, which tend to irritate some people, let's look at the other side of the matter, namely, we (you and I) are not simple, and therefore not fully integral.

We should not forge ahead with this theme of God's unicity without also adding that Christians believe that this simple God is also *triplex*, that is, a trinity. This is a belief that is not shared by Jews and Muslims, who cannot understand or imagine how we can entertain such a bizarre notion. To them, it seems to utterly undercut our monotheism, which it surely does from any other standpoint but faith. But since the fourth or fifth centuries, when these matters were sorted out by several church councils, Christians have insisted that God is both one and three. However, his threeness really does not come into this discussion of simplicity.

Since God is utterly one and simple, and we are utterly complex and complicated, how can we approach such a God or relate to him? This was a question that greatly exercised the spiritual writers of the Middle Ages, say, roughly the seventh to the seventeenth centuries. They were acutely aware that not only are we humans unlike God in our natural multiplicity but we are also fragmented because of sin. Due to our disobedience to God, we now find it hard, nay, sometimes almost impossible, to maintain our spiritual integrity. In psychological terms, that also means that we find it hard to focus on God. Clearly, that is a major concern when it comes to prayer. As anyone knows who has seriously pursued a life of prayer, distraction of the mind is a constant struggle.

Many of the Christian mystics of the Middle Ages addressed the problem of spiritual fragmentation in a rather radical fashion. Not only did they search for ways of curing the distractions of the wandering mind, they even advised that the most effective prayer is "imageless." This might seem self-defeating, since the goal is union with the divine image. But to the mystics, human, psychological images themselves are part of the problem since they tend to be fragmentary and fragmenting. So then, pray without them, say the medieval mystics. But that is far easier said than done.

This spiritual problem of how a disjointed soul can focus on the perfectly simple and univocal God—this issue is perhaps not quite what it might seem on the surface. For it is not just a typical problem of epistemology, where an agent seeks to know an external object. Christian spirituality from the very beginning has made the extraordinary claim that God is not just apart from us but also *within us*. This astonishing idea is usually based on the text of Genesis 2:26: "Then God said, 'Let us make man in our image, after our likeness.' " That simple, straightforward sentence has a world of possibility if we are looking at it in the right way. Without any special interpretation, it seems to say that God made man *like himself*, which tends to overturn our earlier suggestion that God is simple and we are multiple.

Yet the early commentators like Gregory of Nyssa and Origen knew very well that things are really not that simple and straightforward. God is simple all right, but we are not always so. To put it another way, our simplicity, unlike God's, is not inalienable. We can and do tend to fragmentation. For example, we do not always follow the will of God, even when we think we know what it is. To state this spiritual problem in terms of Genesis 2:26, we are always in God's image, but not always in his likeness. In terms of rehabilitation, we must strive to regain our intended (by God) condition of resemblance to God. That is just another way of saying that we need to be reunited with God. As is well known, union with God is the main spiritual goal of all persons, not just Christians.

To return to the issue of our fragmentation, it should be clear enough that it is an obstacle to our union with God. As we have seen, the problem is not distance. We are never far from God, or, rather, God is never far from us. But any kind of meaningful union between Creator and Creature must needs involve some kind of homogenization. There needs to be some degree of sameness. Although this very suggestion may shock some pious people, it is nevertheless elementary to much classical spirituality. For example, the Greek church often talks of *theosis*, the transformation of people into gods. That in itself is absurd and even heretical, but the underlying idea is not: we need to be gradually deified.

Is there anything in the Rule of Benedict that even vaguely hints at these things? Not very much! Benedict is notoriously reticent on spiritual matters, at least those having to do with mysticism. Still, there are a few texts that offer some hope. For example, in RB Prol.9, we find the following passage: "Let us open our eyes to the deifying light, and let us listen with astonished ears to the warning of the divine voice, which daily cries out to us." The key term of interest for us here is "deifying" (*deificum*). Now I have to admit that this term is usually not rendered thus by RB translators, including T. Kardong! Strictly speaking, *deificum* can mean "made by God" or "making godly," and most translators prefer the former. One wonders if Greek translators would have the same tendency if faced with this sentence.

The context of this rather evocative usage by Benedict has to do with spiritual transformation. The Prologue of RB appears to be taken from an early Christian baptismal homily, where an (adult) convert is exhorted by the priest to wake up to the new reality he is coming into. Adapted to the monastic postulant, the abbot is urging the candidate to wake up and enter the new monastic existence fully aware of what is happening. Many of us tend to be in a kind of daze on such occasions, but at least this text wants us to work toward a return to the image and likeness of God.

Another passage in Benedict's Rule that has some possibilities in this direction seems to occur in RB 52, on the oratory of the monastery. It seems best to quote this little chapter in its entirety:

> [1]The oratory should be in fact what it is called, and nothing else should be done or stored there. [2]When the Work of God is finished, they should all leave in deepest silence and show reverence for God. [3]Thus will the brother who may wish to pray by himself not be hindered by the thoughtlessness of another. [4]But if someone perhaps wishes to pray privately at some other time, let him simply go in and pray, not in a loud voice but with tears and full attention of heart. [5]Therefore, whoever is not busy with this kind of work is not permitted to remain in the oratory, as the place is called. For the prayer of another should not be disturbed.

Probably there is not much that will strike the reader as germane to our topic of simplicity. There is, though, the innocuous little adverb *simpliciter* in verse 4, which might merit a second look. What is the point of this remark of Benedict? What is the alternative to "simply" going in to pray? Perhaps it is a sly criticism of people who insist on making prayer something complicated. The comment that jumps to mind in this regard is that of the English Abbot John Chapman: "Pray as you can, not as you can't!" As I read Chapman's famous piece of advice, the important thing with prayer is to avoid a lot of thinking and plotting. Just go in and do it!

Actually, there are other comments here that run in the same direction. The monk is sternly forbidden to indulge in an elaborate rigmarole of loud prayer formulae. Implied is more than the author's obvious distaste for elaborate prayer forms. Not only will the praying brother be a nuisance to himself with his "loud prayers," but he will be a distraction to others. Moreover, it seems that this second, social element is the real emphasis of the chapter: "the prayer of another should not be disturbed." Benedict really does not like this kind of behavior. He calls it "thoughtlessness," but I wonder whether that is a strong enough translation for *improbitate*? After all, charity is the highest value of Christianity, and if another practice, even a favorite form of prayer, violates charity, then it is illegitimate.

There is another possibility here. We might miss the seemingly artless remark that Benedict makes in verse 1 about the oratory not being a place for anything else but prayer. He even cautions that it is not to be used as a storeroom. That might appear to be a rather picky or obsessive sort of demand, but I suggest that it is not. We in this country are perhaps not used to churches where a lot of "junk" is allowed to accumulate. But the traveler in Italy will certainly become aware that some churches are badly in need of cleaning, or at least *simplification*. To my mind, the problem may begin with the very elaborate and over-decorated style of architecture that one finds too often in baroque Catholic churches. I seriously doubt whether that is conducive to undistracted prayer.

But there is another phrase in RB 52 that deserves our fullest attention in this discussion: "Pray with tears and full attention of heart." Exactly how tears relate to our present topic may not be too clear. Certainly "full attention of heart" is right on the point. Here is exactly what we are concerned with, and it is clear that it is the real focus of Benedict's chapter and Benedict's chapel. Lest we might suspect that Benedict's mention of tears suggests an emotionalism that is out of place, *intentio cordis* should serve as a corrective to such a mistaken notion. As Michael Casey pointed out in a classic article years ago on this very text, the "heart" was not primarily the seat of emotion for the ancients. Indeed, it might be better to translate *cor* by "will."

I think it is worth stressing this point because I think many people have a sort of inferiority complex when it comes to prayer. Far from bragging about their prayer, they freely admit they find it very difficult. As someone once said, when it comes to prayer we are all beginners. True enough, but at least we should be realistic about the matter. When Benedict counsels "tears" for our prayer, we may think to ourselves that we often are simply not "in the mood" to pray. We go into the chapel, but when we get down on our knees—nothing! What to do then? Someone might say: concentrate! On what? We know we often can manage neither tears nor attention of heart, which can produce a continual sense of failure.

But we should also remember that "success" in this matter is not like success in other matters. Prayer is not just communication with God but also a gift of God. He gives it to whomever he wishes and in whatever way he wishes. To return to the mystics for a minute, they knew all about the gratuity of prayer. They knew, for example, that we can deliberately conjure up all kinds of images of God for the purpose of prayer. But they also knew that the best prayer, that is, to their minds, imageless prayer, is basically a gift of God. No amount of striving on our part can produce it. We can try to live a life in which we avoid distractions, but in the end, God gives himself to whoever he wishes. Just go in and simply pray!

Chapter 8

Perfection

The overall thesis or leitmotif of these essays on the Rule of Benedict is that the author, that is, Benedict, started out his writing project very much under the thrall of the Rule of the Master. But as time goes on, or at least toward the end of the Rule of Benedict, the author seems to find his own legs in that he relies less on the RM and develops his own teachings. My general feeling is that Benedict was a better monastic legislator toward the end of his Rule.

Yet we have also seen that this rule of thumb should not be taken as absolute. Benedict finds ways to make his own mark in the early pages of the Rule; furthermore, there are passages in the last chapters that strike me as less than Benedict's best. As a good example of this exception to the general rule I would propose RB 73, "That the Whole Fulfillment of Justice Is Not Laid Down in This Rule. "

The basic teaching of RB 73 is simple enough: Those who follow the Rule that precedes ought not to think they have done anything great; there is a higher level of monastic perfection still to be attained, and this fuller degree of spiritual fulfillment can be learned by consulting Scripture and the monastic Fathers. Taken alone, this thesis is rather attractive, since it shows the author to be a modest writer and it also leaves matters open-ended. In this sense, RB 73 is quite progressive in tone.

Still, it should be added that the very idea of perfection is problematic. For one thing, it seems to be a new concern for Benedict. The term *perfectio* appears here for the first time in the entire document. Why has he waited so long to introduce it? If RB 73 is an epilogue, as some scholars think it is, then it really should not bring up new matters. Besides that, perfection itself is not a comfortable notion, especially in regard to the spiritual life. To put it succinctly, we know we are not perfect and also that we never will be. So what are we to make of RB 73?

Relation of Epilogue to Prologue

One of the unanswered questions about RB 73 is its relation to the rest of the document. The Latin begins with *Regulam autem hanc descripsimus*, "The Rule, however, which we have sketched out." This opening looks like it continues the previous chapter, but in what way? RB 72 is all about love for God and for neighbor; RB 73 on perfection seems to take off on a new tangent altogether. Personally, I wish Benedict had ended at RB 72.11-12, which is a perfect conclusion to a communal monastic rule. I consider RB 73 a rather ill-advised addition to the document, but I also admit that the job of the commentator is to deal with what the text actually says, not what he wishes it said.

Another possible angle on this question lies in RB 66. That little chapter ends with the interesting stipulation: "We want this Rule read rather often in the community so no brother can excuse himself because of ignorance." Since that is the way some other monastic rules end, it is very possible that RB 66.8 was the original ending. Besides, the Latin is certainly intriguing: *Hanc autem regulam*, which neatly matches RB 73.1, but in reverse.

Since none of these arguments are completely probative, I would take the liberty to add yet another. It seems to me that there is a good deal of similarity between RB 73 and the ending of the Prologue of RB. On one level, there are certain terms like *initium* (beginning), *cursus* (run), and *conversatio* (life) that are found in both RB Prol.48-49 and RB 73. These words also appear elsewhere in the Rule, but they are still notable. But even more convincing is the fact that both of these passages stress the spiritual progress that the monk should make and can make. This notion of spiritual growth in the monk is obviously very important, and we will have occasion to return to it.

So then, our suggestion is that Benedict's epilogue should be considered a companion piece, or a bookend if you wish, to the Prologue. I should admit, however, that this leaves us with an interesting result. It is generally accepted by commentators that the Prologue of RB is aimed at the beginning monk or postulant. That stands to reason. But what about the epilogue? To whom is it addressed? Is it not possible that it too is meant for the fledgling monk or novice? If that were the case, it would go a long way toward answering the question of why Benedict seems to suddenly treat his Rule as rudimentary in this final chapter: "We have sketched out this Rule, so that carrying it out in monasteries we may at least show that we have moral decency and the rudiments of a monastic life" (RB 73.1).

Perfection in the Rule of the Master

As we have noted, Benedict's dependency on the Master basically disappears by the end of RB. That is also true for RB 73; it has no apparent literary connection to the RM. And yet perfection is a rather prominent theme for the Master. It does not have a chapter to itself, as with Benedict, but it forms the basis for the Master's curious teaching on silence in RM 8–9. These are chapters that Benedict has mostly avoided, but it is still worth mentioning them in comparison to RB 73. The basic idea is this: for the Master, the most perfect monk is one who speaks less or hardly at all. On the other hand, the less perfect monk is allowed to at least ask questions or ask to speak.

The very notion of perfect and imperfect monks may strike us as bizarre. Clearly, some monks *are* better than others, at least in some respects. But to set up a formal, rigid category of perfect and less perfect seems so inhuman and inherently dangerous that it is no wonder that Benedict largely ignores it. Since the Master does not seem to even suspect what problems he is creating by such dubious categories, we should at least try to spell them out. The very idea that there are "perfect" monks lies at the heart of the Master's hierarchy of monastic officials. Who should become abbot? Who but the perfect monk? But it seems that for the Master almost all the other monks are hopeless dolts. So where are these perfect abbots to come from?

Moreover, the Master shows no signs of progressive thinking on this matter. Nowhere does he suggest that imperfect monks can become perfect monks. His categories are completely closed. That could be the reason why he seems to offer no prospect of spiritual progress here on earth. He does promise the monks a heavenly reward. Indeed, he twice launches into almost hysterical rhapsodies describing the delights of heaven (RM 3.78-95; 10.92-120). But short of heaven, the Master does not have much to offer the monk. It may not be quite as bad as the scene in a mythical monastery where the monk is reputed to have asked the abbot about his "rights" as a monk. The answer was not reassuring: "You have the right to a Christian burial." Or it could be that the Master thought like a certain abbot who once told me that as far as he could see, monks have no rights, only duties.

Seen in this dismal light, it could be that RB 73 stands as a corrective. Benedict does not want to leave the monk with a stunted notion of his prospects and potentialities. He therefore urges him or her to be sure to consult those Christian documents that do present this life as one of great possibilities. Of course, the Bible itself is exemplary in this regard. First Corinthians 2:9 is a fine text: "What eye has not seen, and ear has not heard, and what has not entered the human heart, what God has prepared for those who love him, this God has revealed to us through the Spirit." This refers to heaven, of course, but it also notes that this heaven is a reward for our spiritual striving. Benedict quotes that text in RB 4.77, at the end of the chapter on instruments of good works.

Benedict also advises his disciple to read the writings of the monastic Fathers, and especially Basil and John Cassian. We will discuss the latter author further on, but at this point a few remarks about "our holy Father" Basil of Caesarea might be in order. Someone who peruses the Long Rules of Basil, or indeed any of Basil's writings, will notice right away that he is very demanding. Indeed, he is so demanding that the newcomer to his writings is tempted to put them aside. For example, Basil insists that someone who violates just *one* of the Lord's commandments violates them all! To his mind, it does no good to keep some of the commandments unless we keep them all (*Long Rules*, Preface 2).

In the face of this implacable moralism, we might throw up our hands and ask, with the disciples of Christ, "Then who can be saved?" But we should not lose heart, for Basil, along with many of the Greek church Fathers, thinks that we have it in us to come up to this standard. Along with Jesus, of course, he insists that it takes divine grace: "With God all things are possible." The Greeks freely admit that spiritual maturity is not arrived at overnight, but they think that real growth is possible. If we continue to plug away at the hard uphill climb, we can expect to arrive at a place where monastic and spiritual life will become a joy and second nature. To quote St. Benedict along these same lines: "Therefore, when he has climbed all these steps of humility, the monk will soon arrive at that perfect love of God which drives out fear" (RB 7.67). This optimistic take on human possibilities may well have been one of the key things Benedict learned from Basil.

Matthean Perfection

Another angle of possible enlightenment on RB 73 can be found in the title of the chapter: "That the Whole Fulfillment of Justice Is Not Laid Down in This Rule." It seems to me that this is one of most curious and fascinating titles in the entire Benedictine corpus. Since we know that the topic of the chapter is perfection, we might well wonder why Benedict brings up *justice* in his title. Is there some connection between these two concepts? There probably is, but it is not immediately apparent. Yet if we take another path of inquiry, namely, to explore whether justice is a keyword in Benedict's Rule, I think we can say that it is.

Of the nine times that Benedict uses the term *justitia*, no fewer than four of them quote or allude to the Gospel of Matthew (RB 2.5; 2.35; 4.35; and 73T). Granted, numbers like this do not mean too much; the question is whether Benedict has the same take on justice as does Matthew. I think the answer to that may well be yes. We should remember that Matthew is the most Jewish of the evangelists, probably even a rabbi. So he knows his Scripture very well, and he uses the Old Testament more than any other New Testament writer.

What is the Jewish notion of justice? It is important to clear away most of our modern ideas of justice before we can grasp the

Jewish concept. For the ancient Jews, justice (*sedekah*) is basically *covenantal*. That means that it is entirely rooted in the tribal relations of the Jews to one another. As such, it is not an abstract value that I owe to everybody. In plain language, justice is what I owe to my brother Jew, because he is a Jew and therefore my brother. This being the case, we can find instances in the Jewish Bible (OT) where one Jew renders justice to another Jew by doing some things that we might consider morally dubious. We might feel that we moderns have risen above the tribal feeling and thinking that pervades this Jewish thinking, but at least we need to face up to what Old Testament justice is really all about.

It is probably accurate to say that some of this tribalism is left behind when justice is invoked in the New Testament, but how much? Let us look at a rather mysterious text like the one we find in Matthew 3:15. When Jesus comes to John the Baptist at the Jordan River to be baptized, John balks at the very idea: "I need to be baptized by you, and you are coming to me?" But Jesus does not bend to that argument; he says: "Allow it now, for thus it is fitting for us to fulfill all righteousness." We might wonder how this text is germane to this discussion, until we learn that the Greek term translated here as "righteousness" (*dikaiosyne*) is the same one used to translate the Hebrew for "justice." So John is referring to justice, and it must be Jewish justice, since both he and Jesus are good Jews.

What does it mean that "all justice must be fulfilled"? Remember, this is the very same language used by Benedict as the title for his final chapter. According to the note in the New American Bible, Revised Edition, which I consider very authoritative, this righteousness/justice refers to God's saving activity, and in the case of Matthew 3:15, the salvation of the whole human race. So clearly, we are faced here with some extremely weighty material. At least we can see that Matthean justice is by no means limited to the individual; it is a corporate concept.

Granted, it cannot be proved that Benedict had the whole Matthean context in view when he wrote RB 73T. Yet, I think we are engaging in legitimate exegesis, and not "over-interpretation," when we look to Matthew for light on RB 73. For example, we might well suspect that our take on "justice" will affect our take on "perfect." In fact, there is at least one more passage in Matthew that seems to point in the same direction. This is the famous line in the Sermon on the Mount: "So be perfect, just as your heavenly Father is perfect" (Matt 5:48). Unless properly understood, this might be seen as the most outrageous demand of Jesus in the whole Gospel. How can he ask us to be like God? Is he trying to crush us?

Yet the context shows clearly enough that he is not trying to intimidate us. Just before Matthew 5:48, Jesus explains quite unambiguously what he means by "perfect": not flawless! This is brought out in Matthew 5:45: "[Your heavenly Father] makes the sun rise on the bad and the good, and causes the rain to fall on the just and the unjust." So what is the point? Simply to insist that the God of Jesus Christ, the one that we are called to be like, is quite inclusive in his love. Indeed, he is so inclusive that he does good to those who do evil. Of course, we know that Jesus elsewhere calls for the same attitude on the part of his disciples and then carries it out in his own passion and death.

To return to RB 73, notice that this also casts Benedict's perfection in a different light. It makes us adjust our first impulse in understanding "perfect," which is quite different from that of Matthew's Sermon on the Mount. Our first understanding of perfect is not inclusion; it is flawlessness. When we hear "perfect," we hear "no mistakes, no errors," even "no sins." It is hard to imagine a sharper contrast than that between "inclusion" and "flawlessness." This may not satisfy someone who is still looking for the exact correlation between justice and perfection, but it should be a good start.

Another Matthean text that can help to loosen up our notions of the kind of perfection urged by Benedict can be seen in Matthew 19:21. In this well-known passage, Jesus engages in a rather probing conversation with a rich young man. This fellow has a lot of goodwill. If he did not, he would not have come to Jesus with the question "What good must I do to gain eternal life?" Jesus answers him with the commandments, which you would think might have satisfied him. But no, "All these I have observed; what do I still lack?" He is really sticking his chin out! "If you wish to be perfect, go sell what you have and give to the poor . . . and come follow me!"

So our keyword "perfect" shows up again in Matthew, and in a very important text, at least for understanding the monastic life. Throughout the history of exegesis, commentators have seen this text as somehow grounding the Catholic religious life. Never mind that there were no monks or nuns in Jesus' time, so Jesus could not have been referring to them here. Still, his demand for radical dispossession for this rich young man seems to be aimed at us monks—except that I am quite sure that it is not! Think about it: radical dispossession really cannot be the heart of Jesus' call to discipleship, at least not for most people. Even if we do not own much, or perhaps do not legally own anything, we still *use* all sorts of things. So whatever dispossession is called for here has to be quite *relative*.

Since this is the only time when Jesus demands dispossession from a follower, we have to suspect that this was a specific and limited case. For this young man, dispossession was the only way forward. He had made very good progress in the moral and spiritual life, but to come closer to Jesus and to salvation demanded complete poverty. Someone might know enough Scripture to remind me that the first Jerusalem community also practiced radical dispossession. In Acts 4:32-35, we are told that the Jerusalem community held all their goods in common. Yet I think that a close examination of that passage reveals that this was *not* a blanket demand made of all the early Christians. There is no other indication in the New Testament that such was the case. Here is another case of seeing the relativity of perfection, so I think Matthew's gospel can help us properly weigh RB 73.

Perfection for John Cassian

A glance at the specialized index of *RB 1980* that details the patristic sources of RB 73 (p. 607) indicates that most of the references are to John Cassian. This is no great surprise, since Benedict himself tells the aspiring monk to study the works of Cassian: "And then there are the *Conferences* of the Fathers and their *Institutes* and *Lives*, along with the Rule of our Holy Father Basil." Although several patristic authors use these titles, "Conferences" and "Institutes" are probably best taken as referring to the writings of Cassian.

Before we ask about Cassian's view of perfection, we might note that Michael Casey once suggested that Benedict's listing of Cassian and Basil in the same sentence could have an interesting resonance. Casey said that Basil is generally taken as a cenobitic writer, while Cassian is more of an anchorite. That is not absolutely true, but it is true enough to leave us with a kind of compendium of monastic literature. It is as if Benedict is advising the monk who wants to probe deeper into monastic wisdom to read both sides of the picture. Or perhaps better, to read *all* sides of the picture. In the 1980s, John Gribomont accused Adalbert de Vogüé of overemphasizing the influence of Cassian on the Rule of Benedict. Gribomont thought he had underplayed the importance of St. Basil as a source of the RB. I agree with Gribomont, but perhaps that is neither here nor there.

The two instances of *perfectio* in RB 73 both occur in the single verse, RB 73.2: "But for someone who is in a hurry to reach the fullness of monastic life, there are the teachings of the Holy Fathers. Anyone who carries them out will arrive at the pinnacle of perfection." The first use of *perfectio* in this verse is obscured by the fact that I translated it "fullness" in my commentary. It is too late to change that now, but it is a good object lesson to me that one should not tamper with Benedict's keywords, even at the expense of monotony. Variety is a characteristic of lively language, but it is not necessarily the sign of a good translation. At any rate, these usages in themselves do not shed any special light on Cassian's overall theory of perfection.

Probably the best place to study that theory lies in Cassian's Conference 11, which is titled "The First Conference of Abbot Chaeremon: On Perfection." This is one of Cassian's shorter conferences, and I think the reason is because his take on perfection is essentially simple: there is no absolute perfection in this world! That is a truism that did not take divine revelation to reveal to the world. It is something that almost everyone has learned by the experience of life, often the hard way. We tend to stumble through life, and no matter how admirable are our ideals, we rarely, if ever, reach them.

This is a lesson that is so important that to miss it is to suffer a crippling character defect called "perfectionism." We don't hear that word too much nowadays, but the reality is far from absent. Some people cannot reconcile themselves to being merely mortal and human. Mistakes for them are a personal affront not to be tolerated, in others and in themselves. And so they are condemned to struggling with a false concept of human possibilities, and especially of their own possibilities. I once met an old Trappist monk who did not act much like a Trappist monk. While I ate breakfast in the guesthouse, he strolled up and down smoking cigarettes. At one point he said something like this: "I used to hate my faults and weaknesses, but now I have come to love them." I almost choked on the grapefruit, but I have never quite forgotten that remark.

For his part, Cassian, in Conference 11.7, invokes a traditional metaphor for spiritual growth. He says there are three levels of fear. The first level is the fear of slaves. They do what they are told to do because they fear that if they do not, they will be beaten or even killed. The second level of fear, says Cassian, is the fear of hirelings. They also do what they are told, but their fear is different. If they disobey, they fear that they will not be paid. Finally, there is a third level of fear, which Cassian calls the "fear of sons." They obey their father, not because they fear a beating or because they fear not getting paid. They obey their father because they love him. For that reason, they fear that they will hurt or grieve him if they refuse to go along with his wishes. There is some question if the third level of fear should really be called fear at all, but the point is clear enough.

We may well prefer the concept of love to Cassian's highest form of fear, and in fact Cassian makes that same point later in Conference 11 (12). But his thesis is the same: there are different levels of love, which only approximate perfect, absolute love. For us humans, there is no attainment of perfect love. We can be granted a share of the divine love, which then does not really belong to us but to God. But our own attainment is always partial, and it always falls short. From this point of view, it was quite unfair for the church of the fifth century to accuse Cassian of "semi-pelagianism." That was a heresy that claimed that human creatures can indeed attain spiritual perfection in this life on their own. Cassian did make high claims for what we can attain, but he never thought it was our attainment alone.

Another way that Cassian expresses his doctrine of relative perfection can be seen in Conference 1, where he talks about the difference between objectives and goals in the spiritual life. He stresses the need to have two kinds of goals, which he calls *skopos* and *telos*. These Greek terms refer to earthly goals and heavenly ones, at least as Cassian uses them. Specifically, he thinks that we need to have limited, realizable goals, and not just the general goal of attaining heaven. It is easy enough to see this in psychological terms; it is encouraging to be able to at least sometimes reach our limited, mundane goals. This can keep us striving ever upward. If we insist on aiming only for the heavenly goal, we may well sink down in discouragement, because we will never reach heaven in this life.

Is Benedict aware of Cassian's overall theory of perfection? He never quotes it in full, but the very fact that he uses so much Cassianic language in this last chapter indicates that this is his basic reference. Even though the final chapter RB 73 might yield a superficial impression that it is urging or demanding absolute perfection from the monk, in its proper Cassianic context that is not what is meant. At the end of his Rule, Benedict wants us to know that we have not arrived at a state of perfection where we can rest on our laurels. Spiritual perfection is strictly open-ended. There is always something more to be learned. Love can always grow and develop into something more: "Love never ends."

Chapter 9

Brotherhood

In Benedict's chapter titled "Rank in the Community," we come upon a curious verse that reads like this: "The seniors are to call their juniors by the title 'brother,' but the juniors should call their seniors 'nonnus,' which means 'reverend father.'" Our first reaction to this exchange might be to dismiss it as something from a bygone age of formality. Modern people, at least modern Americans, are not big on titles. But beyond that, our democratic heritage and culture probably makes us wonder why these two monks, even though they are "senior" and "junior," could not treat each other as equals. The very idea of special titles designating rank does not come natural to us. What is the background for this hierarchical nonreciprocity, to give it the fanciest label possible?

Context of RB 63

Benedict's chapter on rank probably does not rank very high in current studies of his monastic Rule. We rarely see it quoted, yet we need to examine it closely in order to situate the whole question of brotherhood in the Rule. Benedict makes it clear that he is establishing a new order, something quite different from the usual order in society. He means to arrange his whole community by rank, and that rank is essentially determined by time of entry. In order to make sure we do not misunderstand him, he spells the whole thing out: If you arrive at the monastery at noon and I come at one o'clock, then you are senior and I am junior. Moreover, this order is not for just a day but for life. Each of us is given our place in the monastic, cenobitic order of Benedict.

When I first came to the monastery, before Vatican II, I found that this elaborate system of ranking was carried out to the letter. The monks kept to their order of seniority in many situations: in choir, at table, and even in receiving Holy Communion. Everybody was quite conscious of his position in regard to everyone else, because he could see who was standing on each side of him. It was one of the few prescriptions of the Rule of Benedict that we kept to the letter. Hardly any monastery still functions this way, but that is another matter.

Let us step back a bit and reflect on the overall significance of Benedict's radical new order. I call it "radical" because it sets aside the usual order in human society. In traditional society, it is the birth order that counts. Elders are accorded honor by the younger members, and not because they are necessarily wiser. They are deferred to *because* they are elders. If I go away to college to study science and come home, I do not contradict grandpa if he says the earth is flat. But in most postindustrial societies, scientific learning now reigns supreme. Nowadays it is "objective" knowledge that counts; before it, all else must give way.

For his part, Benedict puts aside these ordinary criteria and sets up his own system of mutual relations, based on date of entry. This system cuts through traditional ranking based on status or economic standing. For us, these may not seem like very important considerations, but in the ancient world, they were revolutionary. Once you entered the monastic order, it did not matter whether you were a prince or a peasant. No doubt your education would fit you for certain roles, including leadership, but fundamentally, all traces of "caste" were cast aside, to make a bad pun.

Although Benedict's order of ranking ran against the grain of ancient society, it was not a new idea on his part. From the very beginning of Christian monastic history, at least communal monastic history, date of entry always trumped date of birth or any other criterion. Thus the earliest cenobitic rule, that of Pachomius (*Pr.* 1, 13), also goes by date of entry, as does the earliest Western rule at Lérins in France (*RIVP* 2.11; 4.4). As we will see later the sole exception to this method of arranging monastic relations was the Rule of the Master.

Fraternity in the Early Church

If we cast our nets wider, and also deeper, to study brotherhood (fraternity) in the New Testament and the early church, what do we find? Certainly this was a key concept among both the Jews and the Christians. Like all tribal societies, the Jews thought in terms of kinship. Here is a typical text: "If there is among you a poor man, one of your brethren, in any of your towns within your land which the Lord your God gives us, you shall not harden your heart or shut your hand against your poor brother, but you shall open your hand to him, and lend him sufficient for his need, whatever it might be" (Deut 15:7-8, RSV). Whether this ideal was always carried out, it was the ideal accepted by all Jews.

The Christians, like good Jews, thought along the same lines. They too considered their fellow Christians "brothers" but also had a tendency to treat others less generously. The Gospel of Jesus, however, is more radical than the Jewish Torah, so we find texts that undercut the notions of family and brotherhood. For example, in Mark 3:33-35, Jesus is reminded that his mother and brothers are waiting for him outside. His rejoinder is sharp: "Who are my mother and my brothers? . . . Whoever does the will of God is my brother and sister and mother!"

Another important text for our study occurs in Matthew 23:8-9: "As for you, do not be called 'rabbi.' You have but one teacher, and you are all brothers." That "one teacher" is Jesus, and no doubt Matthew implies that the disciples are all brothers because they share divine sonship with Jesus, as sons of his heavenly Father. Lying behind this particular quote is Matthew's apparent wish to differentiate Jesus' disciples from those of the rabbis. They had a lot in common, but not everything. But that is a detour we should not make at this point.

While the New Testament refuses to make an idol of family relations, it does not hesitate to use the language of brotherhood in the most profound theological connections. For example, after his resurrection, Jesus says to Mary Magdalen: "Stop holding on to me, for I have not yet ascended to the Father; but go to my brothers and tell them, 'I am ascending to my Father and your Father, to my God and your God'" (John 20:17, NABRE). Considering the emotional circumstances, we might hesitate to put too much weight on these remarks of Jesus. But apparently Saint Paul had no qualms: "The Spirit itself bears witness with our spirit that we are children of God, and if children, then heirs, heirs of God and joint heirs with Christ, if only we suffer with him so that we may also be glorified with him" (Rom 8:16-17, NABRE).

So it is quite plain that the New Testament considers our brotherly relation to Jesus Christ and to each other as Christians something beyond the psychological. To use a term that is not much heard in our time, we are ontological brothers to Jesus and each other. Because of our baptism into Christ, we are "children of God." There is scope here for some confusion: we are not sons of the Father in the same sense as the only-begotten Son of God, Jesus Christ. But, as Christian writers like to put it, we are "adopted sons and daughters." For our present discussion, this is the bedrock of Christian brotherhood.

Brotherhood in the Early Church

Given the fact that "brotherhood" or "fraternity" played a crucial role in New Testament thinking and discourse, we should expect that it would continue to do so in the history of the early church. Alas, that does not seem to be the case. In an article titled "Fraternité," published in the famous French *Dictionnaire de Spiritualité* in 1964, the young German theologian Josef Ratzinger, later Pope Benedict XVI, combed through the evidence of the first six or so centuries of Christianity. He was looking for instances of Christians calling each other "brother," but he found very little evidence.

One New Testament text that would seem to aid his case is this: "As you did it to the least of my brothers, you did to me" (Matthew 25:40, NABRE). Many modern New Testament scholars claim that "the least of my brothers" is not a social reference but instead a kind of code name for fellow Christians. As such it would be a good candidate for early Christian nomenclature. As for Ratzinger, however, he does not agree. "The least of my brothers" is any disadvantaged person, not a fellow Christian.

The Christian use of "brother" did not fade away everywhere. In North Africa, it turns up in a rather unfortunate situation that is usually labeled the Donatist controversy. After the great persecution of about 250, some of the Christians refused to be reconciled with other Christians who had caved in to their tormentors. They were led by a man named Donatus, and they formed an intransigent block of schismatics who basically denied communion to anyone who disagreed with them. For almost two hundred years they refused to even recognize the rest of the Christian Church.

The Orthodox Catholic bishops of North Africa struggled to convince this stubborn group of their error with all kinds of arguments. Optatus of Milevis (died AD 400) based his argument on baptism: If they are baptized in Christ Jesus, they are, like it or not, *brothers* of the Christians all over the world. They can deny episcopal collegiality but not basic membership in the same spiritual family. Despite the theological profundity of this argument, it did not dent the intransigence of the Donatist fanatics.

Bishop Augustine of Hippo also had his troubles with the Donatists, even calling down the civil authorities against them. But mostly he, like Optatus, endeavored to convince them with biblical arguments: "There are those who hate you . . . even if they do not wish to be your brothers, you should still say to them: you *are* our brothers!" Scholars think that this is a version of Isaiah 66:5. It is not like any version in the Bibles at my disposal, but I recognize that this is the most solid argument for Christian brotherhood.

One other interesting usage of "brother" in early Christianity occurred in the writings of John Chrysostom, a monk from Antioch who became an important bishop. He was quite unhappy with the custom of his time, which called monks, but not other Christians, "brother." He bitterly deplored the narrowing of the concept of fraternity down to the company of monks. To quote Ratzinger:

> Chrysostom deliberately opposed the contemporary custom and forcefully declared that the New Testament understood "brother" to mean Christian and not monk. A monk who is only a catechumen is

not a "brother," whereas a baptized person who lives in the world *is* one. "For what makes one a brother? The bath of a new birth and the power to call God 'Father.'" (*Dictionnaire de Spiritualité* 5.1153c)

But let us not forget our central problem in this essay: Saint Benedict was not content to call all of his monks "brothers." He knew well enough that that was their most exalted title as Christians, yet he preferred the language of hierarchy, which calls some monks "father" instead of brother. Why is this? Because I am trying here to prove a negative, always a slippery proposition, I must remain in the realm of conjecture. Still, I would like to propose an intriguing possibility.

The Rule of the Master

Do I need to rehearse the dependency of Benedict on the Rule of the Master? There can be no doubt they are intimately connected, since the two texts run almost parallel for the first ten or so chapters. But when we get beyond that initial stage, the relationship is less obvious. For example, in regard to RB 63.12, which we are specifically studying, there is no parallel in the Rule of the Master. Indeed, there is almost no discussion at all in the RM concerning "order in the community."

Yet at least one passage of RM does refer to the question of *rank* (or order) in the community. The title of RM 92 reads as follows: "Prohibition of Honor and Rank below the Abbot." This is intriguing, to say the least, but it is also a complete negation of our point. We will need to see further on why the Master will not accord a rank to anybody in his community. Suffice it to say here that this is no slip of the pen: the Master really does mean to create a community *without rank*.

Why does he do this? It all seems to go back to his method of choosing a successor to the abbot. There is no doubt that this is a major issue for him. In fact, he has devoted one huge chapter (93) at the end of his Rule to the question. As we have said, his system is dynastic: the abbot chooses his own successor. Unlike the Rule of Benedict (RB 64.1-2), there is no election of the abbot by all the members. Although it does not tally with our democratic notions, dynasty in itself is not against the monastic tradition. The first cenobitic community, namely, that of Pachomius, was governed by that structure. And recently, at the famous community of Taizé in France, Prior Roger Schutz chose his own successor.

As for the Master, he does not leave the matter vague but attempts to detail every aspect of it. He tells the abbot to keep an eye out for likely candidates for abbatial succession. They should be characterized by perfect obedience and docility. He goes even further: the monks are told that if they wish to be chosen abbot, they should make sure to appear perfectly obedient and docile in front of the abbot. In case the incredulous reader doubts that the Master could be so crass, consider RM 92.48-49:

> If then, as we said above, the abbot leaves everyone's rank undetermined and he sees all exerting themselves in their desire to attain to this honor some day, they will eagerly compete with one another to implement what is of God so that their good deeds may make them acceptable for appointment.

Notice here that the Master considers the abbacy to be primarily an *honor*, whereas anyone who has borne this burden knows that it is also a heavy responsibility. Not surprisingly, the Master soon finds himself entangled by the coils of his own idiotic arrangement. If the abbot names his successor, how should the latter behave? Perfectly! Otherwise, he must be summarily deposed and subjected to shaming. What if the abbot appoints a successor on his deathbed—but then does not die on schedule? Too bad for the designated successor! From now on he must live under the most intense scrutiny, so much so that it must almost be considered a death sentence.

One of the pernicious side effects of this bizarre arrangement is to create a community in which no one but the abbot has any status. One wonders, then, how any one of these downtrodden monks will suddenly achieve abbatial potential simply by being designated the successor. This may seem an essentially impractical discussion, but in fact some of our contemporary communities seem to find themselves in precisely this condition, with no one willing or able to assume abbatial responsibility.

Benedict's Solution

Before we descend too far into the morass of the Master's strange and unworkable world, let me insist that Benedict does not follow it. And one way that he avoids the Master's mess is to make a wide detour around the Master's program of leveling. Much as we might suspect that a good cenobitic order might require a good deal of equality, and it really does, still, Benedict probably can see that this kind of thinking has proven disastrous for the Master. For if no one has any status but the abbot, this in effect eliminates the secondary authority needed in every community. To have only one really responsible person is to court trouble, for it loads too much responsibility on one person, and it also fails to prepare others for responsibility.

I think that Benedict insists on *differentiated* status among his monks for this very reason: not all are the same in their gifts. Typically, Benedict will create a basic structure of equality, but then immediately qualify it. Here is an example: "[The priest] must always keep to the rank of his entrance into the monastery, except for liturgical functions or if he is promoted by the wish of the abbot or the choice of the community because of the merit of his life" (RB 60.5-6). The equalizing element is entrance into the community, but this "objective" factor is fine-tuned by the intervention of the abbot and/or community.

So it seems to me that Benedict has been more or less forced by the bad example of the Master to steer a wide berth around some elements that could have been valuable to him. In the case we are discussing, he could have opted for the basic Christian title of brother for all his monks, even the abbot. Indeed, some contemporary Benedictine communities insist on calling their superior "brother," whether he is a priest or not. Benedict, however, falls back on the arcane and obscure title *nonnus* for a senior monk, and probably for priests as well. He uses the title "lord and abbot" once (63.13), but he does not insist on it. It is never heard in our monasteries, except perhaps ironically.

To conclude with my original question as to why Benedict tells his monks to address each other with different titles, depending on date of entry: I can understand it but I still don't like it. It seems to me that cenobitic, communal monastic life is better served when the members call each other "brother," or even by their simple names. Benedict forbids this, but I wonder whether he would do so in our circumstances. In our present world of individualistic achievement, and individualism, we have less need of differentiation than of bonding elements. Simple address is a good means of bonding.

Chapter 10

Tardiness

Modern nonmonastic readers of this book, if there be any, may be surprised that the author has chosen tardiness and/or promptness as a topic for a whole chapter. The reason for this is simple: Benedict also stresses the topic and even devotes an entire chapter to it (RB 43). As an ethical and cultural theme, tardiness probably does not rate very high in modern estimation. It is doubtful whether the ancients took it much more seriously. Furthermore, certain personalities and temperaments have very little aptitude for promptness. It is well known that in certain cultures, it is absolutely bad form to come on time for things. Anyone who wants to function happily in that culture has to come to terms with that.

Apparently, Benedict was not someone who could be at peace with tardiness. When he wrote his Rule, he did not hesitate to lay out a fairly elaborate and stringent system of regulations aimed at curbing tardiness, if not eradicating it altogether. Was that just an aspect of his personality? Probably not. If we remember that he was much influenced by an earlier rule written by the anonymous Master, we can look there for the same trait. When we do, we find that the Master devotes at least three short chapters to promptness (RM 54, 55, 73). So Benedict is following the earlier tradition in this matter.

From the standpoint of technical, comparative literary study of RB, this is a godsend. For when we examine both rules closely, we find that Benedict has made several adjustments that serve as a window into his particular take on tardiness. We find, for example, that Benedict, for all his insistence on promptness, is not fanatical about it. He realizes that it is by no means equal to godliness. Therefore, he avoids making draconian arrangements to combat it.

Besides the fact that Benedict has devoted so much space to this question, we also find it interesting from a theoretical standpoint. Tardiness is a behavioral problem, and as such it has to be kept in proper perspective. It is not exactly close to the core of a person's essential morality or holiness. In other words, some very good people have a hard time being on time. For years in our monastery, a certain monk came slightly late to almost all community exercises. No one seemed to mind very much, but then one day he was elected abbot. Now what? He proved he was not incorrigible: he never came late again!

Behavior is not unimportant. In fact, behavior is of vital concern in a monastic rule. A monastic rule (*regula*), at least in the classical sense, is primarily a code of behavior, a way that monks should live. Such a code can also be called a *customary*, if it pertains to a single monastic community. But a rule as such is a set of concrete actions and arrangements meant for a group of monks. With the most famous ancient rules, such as the Rule of Benedict and the Rule of Basil, these practical regulations are usually attributed to a certain founding abbot or monk. But the key concept is lived-out behavior.

This means that monasticism, at least as we understand it in the Catholic Church, is not simply a set of ideas or ideals. While it is true that some monastic rules, perhaps most of them, do contain a certain amount of theory or theology, because all these rules are religious, they are not primarily theological treatises. The most influential historical rules, including the Rule of Benedict, contain a judicious mixture of theory and regulation. But we can also say that without a practical monastic lifestyle, there is simply no monasticism.

Therefore, a question such as promptness, or the prohibition of tardiness, is by no means out of place in a monastic rule. Benedict does not make much effort to justify his insistence on "coming on time," but that is because he takes it for granted that a monastic rule should legislate such matters. While I am on this point, I might add that I consider *reverence* the primary reason why monks should come on time. Whether the object is God or our neighbor, we do them no honor by coming late. We don't know exactly how God feels about this matter, but we do know that habitual tardiness is irritating and disruptive in the monastic community.

RB 43: Those Who Arrive Late for the Divine Office or for Table

Benedict's teaching on promptness is found mainly in RB 43, which is part of a cluster of chapters (43–46) on satisfaction for faults. Right away we might note two things: First, the fact that Benedict devotes a whole chapter (and not a tiny one either: nineteen verses) to this topic indicates that he takes it seriously. Second, the material on satisfaction for faults comes much later than the chapters on faults (23–30). There could be many reasons for this, but at least this separation creates a psychological gap: there should be no great haste in clearing the abbot's desk of the problem of faults, as we see in the Rule of the Master (RM 13 and 14) where the discussion of reparation comes immediately after the discussion of faults.

Yet this does not mean that Benedict has created an entirely new treatise on faults and satisfaction. No doubt he has learned from the Master's various teachings on the subject. For example, RM 54 is a beautiful little statement about the need to hurry to the Divine Office: "Like bees going for honey, let the brethren swarm into the oratory in such a way that the holy oratory, which until then was a place of silence, is suddenly filled with the sound of the psalms, and the silence of the holy place moves to the deserted shops and tasks" (RM 54.3-4, translation of L. Eberle). Yet the Master is practical enough to exempt those working too far from the oratory from the Day Hours lest they wear themselves out with rushing (RM 55). Benedict says much the same thing in RB 43.1-2.

It seems to me that the primary influence on Benedict's thinking about promptness and tardiness is probably to be found in John Cassian's Institute 4.12. In that discussion of the topic, the great emphasis is on the promptness of *obedience*. For example, Cassian gives us the memorable picture of the monk who is writing at his desk interrupting his work, even the letter he is crafting, when he hears the signal for some communal function. This is the same idea that Benedict enunciates in RB 43.1. The emphasis is on the need to respond to the summons, which may or may not be convenient.

It is worth stressing the idea that monastic, cenobitic promptness is tied up with obedience. It is not primarily a matter of simply conforming to a timetable. Granted, monasteries do operate on a precise schedule, but the compliance of the monk to the horarium is not a question of personal orderliness. A monk can be quite punctilious about doing everything on time without thereby being particularly obedient. Sometimes obedience requires us to break with the usual schedule to respond to a special need. Further proof that Benedict thinks in terms of obedience rather than punctiliousness can be seen in RB 47, where he makes the abbot the keeper of the monastic bells.

Although this may seem an unnecessarily fine distinction to be making, it can help us to remember that monastic life, even in community and perhaps *especially* in community, is not like a well-run factory. Benedict is sometimes claimed as the first medieval writer to rationalize time and particularly *work schedules*. That may be true, but it is basically accidental. In fact, in RB 48, Benedict bends and tweaks the traditional monastic horarium to accommodate human needs. Monastic time is not primarily clock time; it is wisdom time.

Promptness at the Divine Office (RB 43.4-12)

The first aspect of monastic time that Benedict discusses in RB 43, and the main bulk of the chapter, refers to the Divine Office. The subject is not just any Office but the Night Office, that is, Vigils. This is not surprising, since apparently some of the monks found it hard to rise for the Night Office and get there on time. When we consider that it took place about two o'clock in the morning, we can understand why. But we should also remember that the community retired for the night about seven o'clock in the evening, so they had a decent night's sleep.

In contrast to this, the Master made his monks rise at midnight to pray. They went back to bed after Vigils and had a couple hours' more sleep before Lauds, but they still *broke the night*. Some few monasteries (such as La Pierre qui-Vire in France) still break the night, but the monks will admit that not all of them can maintain this kind of unnatural timetable. If they cannot, they must not force themselves to do it, or it will ruin their health. At any rate, Benedict never asks his monks to break the night.

But Benedict knows well enough that rising for the two o'clock Vigils is by no means easy, especially for some people who are "night people"! Notice how he deals with this ascetical problem. Instead of fulminating against the habitual latecomers, he instructs those leading the Office to carry out the first psalm (94) "very slowly and with pauses." In other words, he accommodates himself to the latecomers, nay, he even seems to conspire with them. This is a passage of the Holy Rule that should be carved on one of the pillars in the monastic choir, if such exist.

It certainly undermines any mythical picture of Benedict as a martinet! It also seems to rule out fussy punctiliousness in regard to the monastic schedule. Even though he devotes an entire chapter to the issue of coming on time, there is no fanaticism in his thinking. There is another chapter of the Holy Rule, namely, RB 22, that takes us into the common dormitory where the monks are rising from sleep. There again the author acknowledges that it can be a hard time of the day for some people: "The monks will always be on the ready to rise without delay at the signal. . . . They should hasten to beat one another to the work of God—of course with all decorum and modesty. . . . Moreover, when they rise for the work of God, they should gently encourage each other to offset the excuses of the drowsy." The atmosphere here is basically compassionate and full of the milk of human understanding.

One of the most poignant reminders of ancient rising for Vigils can be seen in the medieval ruins of the French monastery of Fontenay, near Dijon. Here, the dormitory lies directly adjacent to the monastic choir, and they are connected by a long flight of stone steps. What is remarkable about those steps is that they are deeply grooved by six centuries of human feet. It takes no imagination at all to see the brothers trudging down to Vigils in the near-dark, no doubt yawning and blinking, but still trying their best to arrive before the cantor has completed the long, drawn-out invitatory psalm. I found those steps as remarkable as any reminiscence of ancient monasticism that I saw in Europe.

But what if a monk still comes late? What does Benedict do? It might be better to ask what he does *not* do. He does not banish them from choir! He could have done that, and he would have had plenty of historical precedent for doing it, since that is what we find in several of the older monastic rules (RM 73; Cassian, *Inst.* 3.7; *Reg. Macarii*, 14). Instead, Benedict chooses to follow the oldest of all the monastic rules, the Pachomian *Precepta* (8 and 10). In that rule from south Egypt, the great cenobitic founder, Saint Pachomius, has the latecomers sit on a special tardy-bench. Actually, Pachomius demands something more: a dramatic show of submission and contrition indicated by loosening of the monastic belt and habit.

As for Benedict, he does not go in for dramatics. Here we should probably quote his entire regulation:

> If anyone arrives at the Night Office after the Gloria of Psalm 94—and for that reason we want it said very slowly and with pauses—he is not to stand in his own place in choir. But he must stand in the last place or in a place which the abbot has set apart for those who err in this way. Thus they can be seen by him and by everyone until they make public satisfaction at the end of the Divine Office. We have decided they must stand in the last place or apart so they will change their ways under the shame of being seen by all. For if they were to remain outside, there might be some among them who would return to bed and sleep, or sit themselves down outside and gossip, giving the devil an opening. No, they should come in; and then they won't lose everything and will improve for the future. (RB 43.3-9)

This lovely little vignette tells us a great deal about Saint Benedict and about the spiritual atmosphere at his time. We should note, for example, the mention of "shame" in regard to the latecomer. He must sit in a special seat, probably the last one in choir. Everybody knows why he is there: he has come late again!

One time years ago there was a monk in our congregation who could not get himself to the morning Office on time. Day in and day out he was late and so he was notorious, even to himself. Now it was the custom at that time for latecomers to "kneel out," which meant kneeling in the middle of the choir for the short space of a Pater and an Ave to show some sign of contrition. One morning, though, this particular monk came on time. But so habituated was he to "kneeling out" that he plopped down in front of the abbot in the usual fashion. "Go to your place," hissed the abbot. "You are on time!"

To return to the idea of "shame," it is not a concept that our society makes much of. But in most ancient cultures, shame was a major social category. People placed a great deal of importance on public appearance. In the Mediterranean basin, for example, it is even felt that all of life basically consists in avoiding shame and increasing one's honor. Obviously, to be formally seated on the "shame-bench" in the monastic choir was something to be assiduously avoided.

Yet this form of shame did not necessarily imply moral culpability. This fact is brought out by the curious fact that one "knelt out" even if one had a perfectly valid reason for coming late, perhaps under holy obedience. Indeed, sometimes we had the strange spectacle of a whole group of monks kneeling out for missing Office because they had been assigned to do substitute parish work. Whether that is what Benedict would have wanted, I have no idea, but I do think that kind of anomalous custom eventually caused most monasteries to simply drop kneeling out.

We might also remark on the fact that Benedict seems to place great importance on one's *place* in the choir. The idea is simple enough: if you are not in your place on time, you risk losing your place. At first, you will lose it temporarily, but eventually, you could lose it altogether. This is another way of talking about *excommunication*. Not ecclesiastical excommunication, which means banishment from the sacraments. This is internal, monastic excommunication, of the sort that is rarely ever practiced in our monasteries any more. Since we live in such a different culture, it is questionable whether these penal customs should be put into actual practice among us. But they still have a good deal of meaning.

Promptness at Meals (RB 43.13-19)

The second place and occasion where Benedict demands promptness, and punishes tardiness, is community meals. This is expected, since for him and for the whole ancient church, meals were very much comparable to official liturgy. As an example of their connection, consider that blessings for the kitchen servers are given in the oratory, not the refectory (RB 35.15-18). Therefore, meals have a quasi-sacred quality for Benedict.

As with the Divine Office, Benedict does not here banish offenders entirely. Those who come late, that is, after the prayers before meals, are not entirely deprived of food. Rather, they are to eat later than the rest of the community. Moreover, the author spells out precisely what that means: if the community eats at noon, they eat at three o'clock in the afternoon; if the community eats at three o'clock, they eat in the evening. Furthermore, monks are not to leave meals early. If they are not present for the closing prayers, they are guilty of the same offense and subject to the same punishment.

It is interesting that unlike tardiness at the Divine Office, Benedict punishes this fault at meals only if it is the fault of the offender. There are many jobs in the monastery that make it hard or impossible for the brothers to come on time for meals. This kind of tardiness can irritate cooks: an insane sister cook once poisoned five of the hospital sisters because they habitually came late to meals. As for Benedict, he tries to be more understanding.

But his relative mildness regarding this fault should not be taken as an indication of his lack of seriousness. Community meals were for him a major event of life for the group and therefore to be protected against disintegration. To do that, he knew he had to defend the solidarity of the group. Once people start wandering in and out of meals at random, the meal structure itself begins to come apart. Modern monasteries often allow some informality in regard to some of their meals, according to circumstances. In a culture where family meals are under acute stress, the monks should function as something of a bulwark of sanity and corporate health.

Chapter 11

Shame

Shame is not a prominent theme in modern thinking and talking. We all know what it feels like, and we all would like to avoid it, but we don't want to think too much about it. In recent years, though, this topic has achieved some prominence in spiritual writing. For example, certain biblical scholars such as Bruce Malina have pointed out that shame was an intrinsic part of everyday life in ancient Israel. Unlike our own western, northern culture, where everything seems to happen indoors and in private, in Jesus' day life was lived out in the streets. And, says Malina, social life largely consisted of the effort to increase one's honor and decrease one's shame. Using this interpretive lens, many of the encounters of Jesus with his neighbors, the people he meant to save, take on a new significance.

Of course, some psychologists will immediately interject that shame is by no means restricted to ancient Israel. They insist that shame is part of the makeup of every last human being; indeed, it is distinctive of the human person: animals feel no shame. From this point of view, shame is not a tragedy or even a weakness. It can be a condition of terrible suffering, as when a person commits an act for which he is bitterly sorry. But there is also healthy shame that seeks to draw a veil over that which needs to be covered. So shame is a fairly broad category that can include virtual contradictions.

Furthermore, moralists and psychologists point out that shame can cover a multitude of very different sins. For example, when I inadvertently step on someone else's toe and they cry out with indignation, I instinctively feel remorse. I did not mean to do it, and it cannot be condemned as a serious moral failing. Perhaps this feeling should be labeled "guilt" rather than shame. But whatever the label, I am better off putting the incident behind me and not brooding over it. The other person's toe may still hurt, but I should not lie awake worrying about it.

On the other hand, there is shame that cannot and should not be so easily bypassed. In this case, the feeling is much deeper and much less localized. For whatever reasons, I feel bad about my personal inadequacies, and questions such as "Does anyone actually love me?" become acutely painful. Or it could be that we are not even able to formulate such questions. The shame is too deep for words; nevertheless, it may be crippling my life. This is the kind of personal suffering that spiritual directors and psychiatrists deal with every day. Their job is to help people articulate these feelings in the hope of uncovering the "real problem."

It may be that the well-adjusted person finds this discussion basically alien because she does not think she feels any shame at all. But is this really a sign of well-adjustment, or is it rather a sign of spiritual obtuseness and shallowness? For example, is it the church's job to convince people of their sinfulness and thus their shame? That could be the impression we get from a writer such as Paul of Tarsus, who hammers away on this point in his famous letters to the new Christian churches. He tells them that they were under the power of sin and death, but now they have been set free by the saving grace of the Lord Jesus Christ. Therefore, they ought to be joyful and grateful to God for such a healing of shame.

As for St. Benedict, he starts out his Holy Rule in much the same fashion. He is not quite as dramatic or blunt as Paul, but he makes the same point: "Willingly accept the advice of a devoted father and put it into action. Thus you will return by the labor of obedience to the one from whom you departed through the inertia of disobedience" (RB Prol.3). So the newcomer to the monastic life is plainly told that she must make an about-face since she is mired in a condition of spiritual sloth and hopelessness. Unless she can accept this diagnosis and open herself up to serious conversion, the monastic life is not for her. In other words, the aspirant is urged to acknowledge the deep spiritual shame that is holding her back.

Actually, Paul does not mention the word "shame" very much, nor does Benedict. But if we think carefully about what shame entails, then we can look beyond the term to the reality of shame and its healing. When we do that, things may look quite different. In what follows, I lift up certain passages of the Holy Rule to examine them more closely and to study them precisely as "shame-texts." When we do that, we may find a whole new world, a world we did not know existed.

RB 23: Public Shaming

Benedict begins his rather extensive regulations on punishment in RB 23 with a carefully thought-out procedure to be employed in correcting an erring monk. The idea is quite simple: First, he should be approached in private by a few seniors and admonished to change his ways. If he ignores this gentle and considerate warning, then he should be brought before the whole community and rebuked. Should he prove obdurate even to this public admonition, then he is to be subject to "excommunication." And if even that does not make an impression, he is to be expelled from the community.

Someone with a rudimentary knowledge of the New Testament will realize that this is essentially the same program as that given in Matthew 18:15-17. There too we find a progression from the private to the public, and there is also the threat of a dire penalty if the culprit resists all warning. In both instances there is awareness that private admonitions are less painful to most people than public rebukes. But in both cases, there is a real possibility of a public shaming before the whole community.

In traditional monasticism, at least in the West, this kind of discipline was carried out in the so-called *culpa*. Here the individual was encouraged to confess his or her transgressions before the whole group, with some kind of forgiveness soon to follow. But in its more extreme forms, *culpa* took the form of *accusations* by confreres, which the individual was expected to acknowledge and atone for. Needless to say, the latter form of *culpa* was subject to abuse, and has mostly been abandoned in our time.

Notice that this system only works where people value *community*. If a person thinks that it is important what the other members think of him, then social pressure can be effective. If he does not, then he will hardly be moved by the threat of group disapproval or even expulsion. It has often been remarked that in our present individualistic culture, monks often seem to excommunicate *themselves* by cutting themselves off from the common life. Clearly, such a person will not be reformed by any threat of exclusion.

With regard to RB 23, we should also understand that the fault or sin in question is of a special kind. This can be seen in the first verse: "If any brother is found to be defiant or disobedient or arrogant or a murmurer, or if he is in any way opposed to the Holy Rule or disdains the directions of his seniors . . ." So what we are dealing here with what is sometimes called nowadays an "attitude." This person has fallen into an adversarial position with the community and its values. This is not just a matter of occasional peccadilloes.

RB 70: Exemplary Shaming

The practice of public shaming, which is hardly ever witnessed in modern monastic life, actually works two ways. Not only is the individual subjected to group pressure, but the group itself is also affected by the experience. This can be seen in Benedict's remarks in RB 70, "That No One Presume to Strike Another Arbitrarily." In this little chapter, which is rarely ever quoted, the author insists that anybody who violates this rule, namely, that no one is to usurp the abbot's role of punishing another monk, that violent person must be publicly rebuked.

But beyond that, Benedict says this about that rebuke: "Offenders should be publicly rebuked so others will experience fear." So it seems that the legislator hopes to accomplish more than a single objective here: not only does he want to scare the individual away from arbitrary acts, he also wants to scare the whole community! The atmosphere must have been something like the medieval city where culprits were publicly executed so that the rest of the population would look on with horror—and learn a salutary lesson. Whether they ever did is another matter. In fact, we know that people crowded to those executions out of bloodlust.

We have to admit, I think, that a chapter like RB 70 speaks of a different world than our own. It is hard to imagine a modern abbot holding public tribunals for punishment so that the rest of the monks can be properly terrified. I remember a scene from my days in boarding school when a student was caught drawing a mustache on a plaster angel. The principal called us all together and stood the offender up in the midst of the group. "I name you public enemy number one!" shouted the boss. As I remember it, most of us thought he mainly succeeded in making a fool of himself. We were not properly terrified.

Still, it cannot be denied that exemplary punishment has a certain logic to it. Presumably people are not entirely impervious to the fate of others. One of the rationales for publicly announced prison sentences is to warn other people away from harmful behavior. If we really are social animals, we will be affected by what happens to other people. If they are let to misbehave with impunity, the danger is that the contagion will spread. Of course, if people secretly admire the culprit, then little is to be gained one way or another.

We might also suggest that RB 70 is particularly sensitive in Benedict's thinking because it is explicitly about usurpation of the abbot's authority. In verse 6, he uses a favorite word of his, namely, "presume." For him, this always connotes an illegitimate taking on of oneself of a role not permitted. Punishment is essentially the abbot's prerogative. Actually, it is probably better labeled his "sad duty," since few abbots like to punish anybody. But when another monk steps into this role without being bidden to do so, Benedict cannot abide it. Such a one must be immediately punished, and the rest should take note. Usually, the monks themselves take care of the problem with remarks such as "Who made you abbot?"

RB 7.62-64: Gestures of Shame

Benedict tends to think in concrete terms about what he wants to see in a monk. This is especially true in regard to shame. Here is a very graphic passage from the twelfth step of humility:

> The twelfth step of humility is achieved when a monk's humility is
> not only in his heart, but is apparent in his very body to those who
> see him. That is, whether he is at the Work of God, in the oratory, in

the monastery, in the garden, on a journey, in the field or anywhere at all, whether sitting, walking, or standing, let his head always be bowed and his gaze be fixed on the earth. Constantly aware of his guilt for sins, he should consider himself to be already standing before the terrifying judgment of God.

It is hard to deny that this is a very moving passage since it seems to make the strongest possible case for humble behavior. "Head bowed and gaze fixed on the earth," such a demeanor is universally read as a sign of humility. Among the Benedictines, it was traditionally taught that "hands under the scapular" was also a sign of humility and therefore the proper way for a monk to comport himself. When a recent abbot told us that this was the right way for us to stand in choir, I was not very happy. But I have to admit that it is the way I usually *do* stand in choir. Perhaps the hands are a distraction for some people?

At any rate, this picture of the humble monk and the way he or she should look, this actually goes a long way back in monasticism. In fact, it goes back to the very beginning. In the earliest rule of all, namely, the *Precepts* of Pachomius, there is a paragraph (8) precisely detailing how the monk is to atone for faults in the community.

> If it happens that during the psalmody or the prayer or the reading anyone speaks or laughs, he shall unfasten his belt immediately and with neck bowed down and hands hanging down he shall stand before the altar and be rebuked by the superior of the monastery. He shall do the same also in the assembly of the brothers when they assemble to eat.

Although Pachomius is even more detailed and graphic than Benedict, it is clear that they think along the same lines. The monk must manifest his guilt by physical gestures, and those gestures are ones that were recognized in ancient culture as signs of contrition. It may surprise us that such public shaming was demanded for such trivial faults as speaking or laughing at the wrong time. But we should remember that that was a much more public culture than ours. It was a society where guilt was dealt with publicly. Apparently the monks expected to be corrected publicly for public faults, no matter how trivial.

Still, we should remember that Benedict's twelfth step and its gestures are not really aimed at guilt. There is no mention of a particular offence. Rather, it is a question of general "guilt for sins." And the context is also very general: "he should consider he is already standing before the terrifying judgment of God." Although this is not a picture that most of us find very comforting, and it is probably not something that most of us dwell on very often, nevertheless, Benedict has the temerity, or the realism, to claim that it should be the monk's general mind-set: we are sinners and so the judgment may be very hard for us. Therefore, we should look the part: we should look properly contrite.

This disposition, which Benedict expects of us from the beginning of the Prologue and throughout the Rule, may be very difficult for us. Beyond the general human difficulty of admitting we are sinners utterly dependent on God's mercy, we have an added degree of psychological aversion to humble behavior. Nowadays we are instructed by almost every self-help book, and also by experienced spiritual directors, that we must not get down on ourselves. A depressed self-concept is regarded as an obstacle to mental health and therefore something to be overcome or avoided. From that standpoint, the twelfth step looks rather different.

Furthermore, there is a fairly fine line between a humble demeanor and a general appearance of moping and depression. Anyone who has lived in close community such as we have in the monastery realizes that individuals who give a hang-dog impression and who are resolutely downbeat, such people are a menace to the morale of the community. Of course, some people *are* subject to mental depression and find it hard to avoid getting down in the dumps. For such people, Benedict's remarks on humility could be a serious problem. At the very least, they have to be employed very judiciously by monastic authority.

RB 73.7: *Rubor Confusionis*

Yet even though some of the deliberate humble behavior suggested by Benedict may be inappropriate in some places and for some people, there is nevertheless a natural expression of shame that is quite involuntary. When we are embarrassed, we blush. In fact, Benedict refers to this phenomenon in his last chapter. In that chapter, he surprises us by insisting that what he has asked in the previous seventy-two chapters is but a bare, rudimentary version of the monastic life. If we want to go deeper, or rather higher, we should consult the great spiritual classics: the Bible and the church Fathers. And when we see the high level of spiritual attainment they expect, we will be positively confounded: "For us lazy monks who lead bad and negligent lives, it is a source of embarrassment and shame." These last two potent words are my rendition of an even more potent Latin combination: *rubor confusionis.*

The Latin is even more graphic because it contains the actual physiological component of human shame, namely, a red face! *Rubor* refers to anything red, but especially a face, and even more especially a blushing face. It is well known that blushing is involuntary. Indeed, it is a phenomenon that some people consider a personal misfortune and actually seek psychiatric help to overcome. Yet it is also thought of as a sign of innocence, or at least innate modesty. In our hypersexualized society, blushing may be disdained as a sign of naiveté or sexual inexperience. But no matter how we interpret it, it usually evidences some kind of discomfort.

In Benedict's eyes, blushing is not a misfortune to be overcome. It is a sign of spiritual health. If we can still blush, we at least have a chance of reformation. And that is what he is about in his last chapter: reformation. He uses this last chance to urge us to not settle for a mediocre monastic half-life. Most of us have managed a comfortable level of monasticity, he says. Now we should go for the real article. It is a daunting, but stimulating, way to end his holy Rule.

RB 46: Externalizing Shame

One of the most remarkable passages in the Rule of Benedict comes at the end of RB 46. In my view, however, RB 46 starts out in a rather unpromising fashion. The author wants us to confess spontaneously every fault we commit, whether the act was deliberate or not. This does bear a worrisome resemblance to taboo thinking, that is, guilt that comes whether we intended it or not. In other words, certain actions are considered reprehensible, even if they were involuntary. This is not usually considered very helpful thinking today, although it probably has its value in a given situation.

But at the end of RB 46, Benedict wants to discuss something else. We must quote him: "If, however, it is a question of a hidden problem of conscience, he should only reveal it to the abbot or one of the spiritual seniors. For they know how to cure their own wounds and those of others, without divulging them in public" (46.5-6). This is very far indeed from taboo thinking! Now the individual has a very intimate and personal problem to deal with. He knows he is wrong, but he needs special help to deal with it. Most of all, he needs an understanding and discreet counselor or confessor in whom to confide.

It is hard to deny that shame is always some kind of factor in the process of avowal of fault and sin. But Benedict wants to mitigate this barrier to forgiveness when he tells us that the counselor or confessor is in the same boat: she or he also "knows how to cure their own wounds" and those of others. Some of the stories of the Desert Fathers give us a precious insight into this spiritual and psychological dynamism when they show the "Father" gently revealing something of his own brokenness as a means of freeing the client to make a candid avowal of sin. This seems to be an especially effective method to heal shame.

Benedict may be making the same point in another passage where it is also a matter of a troubled sinner who needs help to find liberation. In RB 27, he describes the problem of an excommunicated brother whom the abbot cannot seem to reach. In that case, he should send in *senpectae* to assist him with the job. Although *senpectae* is an opaque word, the author provides this definition: "Elderly brothers who know how to comfort the wavering brother as if in secret." There is no mention here of the *senpectae* as "wounded healers," but that could easily be part of their qualification for the job of mediating forgiveness to a brother who is trapped in his shame.

One time our abbot assigned a monk who was a parish priest to another parish. The monk, however, wasn't going anywhere. In fact, he was so determined stay put that he announced it in the daily paper. Since the abbot knew that he himself was part of the problem, he decided to call in the services of the prior, who had a good relationship with the embattled monk on the mission. The prior dutifully drove out in the country to the rural parish and knocked on the door. "Hi, Willy, how are you?" "What are you doing here?" "Oh just driving around. What are you up to these days?" "Busy, busy, packing up to move to Saint Gerties . . ." This was a classic case of finessing and healing shame by indirection. The man needed help escaping his own psychological prison cell.

Chapter 12

Sadness

Tristitia

The topic of sadness might seem like an unlikely one in regard to Benedict and his Rule. Does he even mention it, and if so, does he care much about it? In fact, he mentions it at least ten times, under two different forms: *tristitia* and *contristare*. Of course, mere word counts do not in themselves tell us much, but they can suggest we look deeper. In this case, one of the translators of *RB 1980*, the late Fr. Marion Larmann, found this word so interesting that he wrote a whole article on it (*American Benedictine Review*, 1979).

Larmann noted that, for Benedict, the main issue with sadness is not so much the basic human emotion in itself but the social implication. The verb *contristare* means to make someone *else* sad, and this is something that Benedict wants his monks to avoid. That in itself is significant, because it indicates that his thinking is more social than individualistic. Benedict seems to think that sadness is a special problem in community life, since it affects the morale of the whole group.

One time a Benedictine abbot, when asked how things were in his monastery, said that he felt that low morale was a special problem. Beyond that, he wondered whether low morale was not also endemic to the life of celibacy that monks share with diocesan priests. For whatever reason, he thought the presence of women might brighten things up for his men. No doubt many husbands might scoff at such naïveté, but at least this particular abbot was sensitive to the question of morale in his house.

It is worthwhile to do some cross-checking with regard to *tristitia*. For example, the Rule of the Master treats this term quite differently than the Abbot of Montecassino. For the Master (RM 53), the monk should *cultivate* sadness during Lent. We will see how Benedict thinks very differently about Lent. Nowhere does the Master warn the monks not to sadden each other.

In the Jewish Bible, sadness has a particularly covenantal flavor. If the Jews disobey their covenantal obligations to God, they should not be surprised if they find themselves sad. Here, sadness is seen as a punishment for disobedience, which of course also causes much more serious problems—like the destruction of Jerusalem! But sadness can also drive us back to God, so it is not entirely negative.

The Greek philosophers, and especially the Stoics, had a different take on sadness. To their minds *lupé* was primarily something to be avoided. But they also felt that pleasure was something to be shunned, since it was sure to be followed by sadness. The Stoic ideal was to cultivate a life above any emotion that can distract us and also drag us down. Notice here, that the concern is primarily individualistic, not social.

There are in the New Testament at least two texts that show profound insight into sadness. Paul writes to the Corinthians about his own sadness, and their sadness as well:

> For even if I saddened you by my letter, I do not regret it; and if I did regret it (for I see that that letter saddened you, if only for a while), I rejoice now, not because you were saddened, but because you were saddened into repentance. For you were saddened in a godly way, so that you did not suffer loss in anything because of us. For godly sorrow produces a salutary repentance without regret, but worldly sorrow produces death. (2 Cor 7:8-10, NABRE)

This rather convoluted statement has a lot of emotional overtones, but at least this much is clear: for Paul, sadness can be either helpful or harmful. The criterion is where it leads. If it leads to repentance, then it is "godly," but if not, it is harmful. In 2 Corinthians 2:7, Paul mentions the possibility that excessive punishment might plunge the guilty person into "excessive sorrow." Benedict knows that passage well and in fact quotes it in RB 27.3.

Another New Testament author who thought deeply about sorrow and sadness was Saint John. In his profound reflections on the Last Supper, he has Jesus say the following:

> When a woman is in labor, she is in anguish because her hour has arrived; but when she has given birth to a child, she no longer remembers the pain because of her joy that a child has been born into the world. So you also are now in anguish. But I will see you again, and your hearts will rejoice, and no one will take your joy away from you.

Here, of course, the sadness is particularly intense because it is associated with the often excruciating physical pain of childbirth. But underlying the "mere" agony is the same issue of true sadness and true joy. The sadness of the laboring woman, no matter how difficult, is still temporary. It is also tempered by the knowledge that it is not in vain: a child will be the result. Granted, there is nothing quite like this in Benedict's Rule, but at least it sets some parameters for our thinking.

One of the considerations to be kept in mind when studying sadness in the Holy Rule is the fact that the Latin term *tristitia* has a fairly wide range of meanings. In fact, it can also mean anger. Anger and sadness are not closely associated in English, so we may have trouble bridging this gap, but it still should be kept in mind. Thus a translator must beware of jamming every instance of *tristitia* or *contristare* onto the procrustean bed of sadness. We will be sure to study at least one text where the word connotes anger.

Lenten Joy (RB 49)

Benedict does not mention *tristitia* in his chapter on Lent, but it certainly is an issue there. Older Catholics remember that Lent was always a somewhat lugubrious time in the typical parish. People were urged to do penance, and they were also warned not to have too much fun during this time. Benedict seems to take this into account in his chapter 49, which was modeled on the Lenten sermons of Pope Leo I to the people of Rome. Here is a quote in that direction: "Let (the monk) deny his body some food, some drink, some sleep, some chatter, some joking, and let him await Holy Easter with the joy of spiritual desire."

Several things in this verse (49.7) bear notice. First is the moderation of the statement. Benedict is not urging his monks to squelch *all* their pleasures and fun! Indeed, he apparently takes for granted that they lead a fairly jolly life; why else counsel *less* chatter and joking? Of course, RB 6, "On Silence," seems to want to eliminate all such frivolity, but that is a badly digested take-over from the notoriously misanthropic Master (see RM 8–9). *Pace* Abbot de Rancé, Benedict permits some friendly discourse among the monks.

Actually, this is not a minor issue. The Holy Rule does not arrange for formal recreation periods, but almost all modern monasteries find them quite important, even necessary. It is not natural for a group of people to live cheek by jowl without relating to one another with friendly conversation. The silence of the tomb does not befit a Benedictine monastery. It is a symptom of (bad) sadness and not of communal mental and spiritual health.

"Let him await Holy Easter with the joy of spiritual desire" (RB 49.7) surely calls for comment. The word that catches my eye here is *desire*. Apparently, Benedict wants us to somehow increase our desire during Lent! But the typical message of the church was always to *decrease* our desire, especially during Lent. Now, of course, someone will say that obviously there are different kinds of desire. Indeed, there are, but it may be a rather fine line between them. *Desire* itself is not the problem. It has been pointed out that for Saint Augustine, the whole spiritual life is basically a matter of increasing our desire—for heaven, for God!

Before we leave RB 49, we should not ignore verse 4: "The proper way to (observe Lent) is to restrain ourselves from all evil habits and to devote ourselves to tearful prayer, reading, compunction of heart, and asceticism." This may well look like a recipe for more sadness. Tearful prayer and compunction of heart certainly do not sound very cheerful. But they really have nothing to do with sadness. The tears that Benedict is talking about are not sentimental but moral: We should weep over our sins. And compunction of heart is along the same lines. Our hard hearts need to be periodically pricked to remind us of our spiritual sloth. Lent is meant to energize us.

A Fraught Situation (RB 31.7)

Earlier I made the claim that *contristare* does not always mean "sadden" for Benedict. A text where this seems to be the case can be seen in the chapter on the cellarer, namely, RB 31.7. The verse reads: "If some brother should demand something from (the cellarer) in an unreasonable way, he should not crush him with a rebuke, but deny the obnoxious petitioner in a reasonable and humble manner." Clearly, this is a "fraught situation," with some potential for violence.

To fully understand the context in monastic life, it is necessary to know that the cellarer has a good deal of power. Cenobitic monks, at least as Benedict envisions them in RB 33 where they own nothing of their own, are in a particularly vulnerable position vis-à-vis the cellarer. He or she figuratively and literally holds all the keys, so whatever goods the monk needs must be obtained from this official. Of course, RB 31 makes it abundantly clear that the cellarer only has this power as a delegate of the abbot. There is no separation of powers in the Benedictine system.

To return to our verse at hand, one of the monks has indeed come to the cellarer to obtain what he needs or thinks he needs. But in this case, the cellarer does *not* think he needs it, or perhaps the abbot has told the cellarer not to grant the request. I once lived under an abbot who loved to play "good cop, bad cap." He would grant almost any request, but then call the cellarer and tell him to deny the same request. Looking back, I sometimes wonder why we did not kill that abbot, but those were different times. We were usually quite docile back then.

The petitioner in RB 31.7 is not docile. He (or she) puts up quite a fuss when the cellarer must deny the request. The Latin is rather pungent: *irrationabiliter postulat* (demands something in an unreasonable/insane way). Of course, it is not good to overinterpret these texts, but still we have to be realistic. Some people do not know how to make a "reasonable" request. It may be because they basically do not like to have to beg for what they need, or maybe they just don't know how to express themselves nicely or smoothly. Whatever the reason, in this case the request is made roughly and/ or the refusal provokes an explosion.

Benedict must have found himself in this position more than once. He knows well enough that the human tendency would be for the cellarer to return the insult. After all, the monk really has no business acting so boorishly; he deserves a reprimand. But Benedict also is wise enough to know that a sharp rebuke is probably not helpful in this situation. Most likely, the petitioner simply does not know how to ask nicely for things. What he really needs in this situation is understanding and compassion. So therefore Benedict advises the cellarer to respond gently, not sharply. Here is where humility becomes very practical. Rather than set off an ugly row with a put-down, the cellarer is advised to act nonviolently.

It seems to me that this is a very instructive example for the teaching in RB 31.1 that the cellarer is to be *non-turbulentus* (nonviolent). That may well be a quote from Isaiah 42:4, which is a premier text because it describes the Suffering Servant. We know that this Servant, whoever he was, simply did not return evil for evil. Moreover, it is hard not to think of Jesus himself in connection with this text, who refused to fight back when he was persecuted and even murdered by the state. So the cellarer is expected to hold herself to a very high standard of spiritual maturity.

To address our specific concern, it seems to me that *contristet* here is not to be construed as the antidote to sadness. The petitioning monk (or nun) is not just sad—he is furious! Therefore, in my 1996 commentary (*Benedict's Rule*, p. 258), I translated the verb as "not crush" and not "not sadden." Probably it will not always be possible to "not sadden" people when one cannot accommodate them. But the problem is not just hurt feelings; it is rage. The cellarer should always avoid, if he can, being embroiled in an unseemly row. And the best way to diffuse anger is with calm and humility. That does not mean the cellarer should be a pushover! But there is always a nice way to say no. Benedict says that explicitly in RB 31.14: "Above all else he should have humility, and when he has no material goods to give someone who asks, he should at least return a friendly word."

Sad Workers (RB 48.7)

Here we come to a text where *contristentur* probably does refer to sadness. The situation is interesting:

If, however, the necessities of the place or poverty demand that they themselves work at the harvest, they should not be sad. For if they live by the work of their hands, then they are true monks, as were our Fathers and the apostles. Yet everything should be arranged in moderation because of the faint-hearted. (RB 48.7-9)

When I first came to the monastery (1956), this verse seemed very strange to me. Why should these monks be sad? Don't they know how to work? Are they used to having servants? When we kids complained about work, my parents used to say: "Sorry, but we had to lay the servants off last week!" In fact, the monks of my abbey were and are extremely hard workers, and quite unafraid to get their hands dirty. As one of them said one time years ago: "Me for work!"

Yet times differ and so do cultures. It does appear that in the sixth century—the one in which Benedict lived and wrote—it was not customary for monks to engage in heavy labor. If they had a farm, apparently they hired other people to do the actual farming. Indeed, the Rule of the Master, which is probably very close to Benedict in time and space, does not want the monks to even *manage* farm land. His reason is serious: when they engage in that kind of demanding business, they will not be able to fast (RM 86.25).

For his part, Benedict does not seem to agree. Not only does he not want to spare his monks manual labor, he even claims that such hard work is *necessary* for real monks. It is not clear where Benedict gets this idea. In fact, many monks did engage in hard work, especially in the early days of the movement in Egypt. Moreover, many spiritual writers in all ages insist that serious, demanding work is healthy for monks. As Benedict himself says in RB 48.1, "Idleness is the soul's enemy." Yet there were very good monks, such as those of St. Martin (Marmoutier) who explicitly avoided physical labor. Yet they did work hard at copying manuscripts—which is by no means an easy task!

At any rate, it seems to me that Benedict in RB 48.7-9 is engaging in special pleading. He has a tendency to invoke a mythical golden age when he wants to convince his monks to do something. For example, he claims the old monks did not drink wine (RB 40.6), and that they recited the whole psalter in one day (RB 18.25). Neither of these claims should be taken for cold cash; they are exhortatory, not historical. When Benedict finds it necessary to engage in this kind of exaggeration, it is a sign that he needs to overcome considerable resistance in his readers, that is, his monks.

Nevertheless, it is interesting to notice that even when faced with this kind of reluctance, which many would consider unreasonable, Benedict does not allow himself the luxury of sarcasm or bitterness. Rather, he basically commiserates with them: "they should not be sad." He knows very well that he is saddening them, but it can't be helped. The harvest must be gathered before it rots in the field. It may well be that this kind of occasional very hard work will be quite burdensome for some of the monks. Yet it must be done.

A good place to study this kind of situation is in the famous Rule of Augustine. One special characteristic of that community was the presence of very different social classes. Not only did Augustine's group include the usual tough peasants; it also included some people from very affluent backgrounds. Obviously, hard physical work would be experienced quite differently by such people. The monks from peasant backgrounds would take it for granted, but the pampered rich would find it very hard indeed. In addition, Augustine wrote a whole treatise ("On the Work of Monks") against a monastery in Carthage where they did not want to work.

To return to Benedict, he may be a bit disgusted with his monks who do not want to help with the harvest. He may consider them "wimps," to use a current term. Still, he does not want to cause them undue sadness. He knows that morale is a critical element in the cenobium. If the monks feel overworked, the abbot must take that seriously. He may not be able to spare them because of practical necessities; at least he should be sensitive to their feelings.

Justified Murmuring (RB 35.3)

Our final case of sadness in Benedict's Rule is found in RB 35, "The Weekly Kitchen Servers." This is one of several chapters in this document devoted to dining, and it deals with a corollary of dining, namely, serving. In fact, the chapter begins with one of Benedict's typical programmatic opening statements: "The brothers should serve one another." Before I go further, let me get something off my chest. Nowadays, in the typical American monastery, the brothers do *not* serve one another, at least at meals.

For various reasons, what we usually find in our dining rooms is self-service. Of course, self-service has certain advantages, especially that of convenience in many situations. In my own monastery, we introduced self-service when we no longer had enough (or any!) novices to do the table-waiting. That may be a very practical reason for self-service, but it does not really solve the problem. Benedict wants, Benedict demands, mutual service. I would almost be willing to declare that mutual service is at the heart of cenobitism.

Be that as it may, our topic here is a bit different: "Let help be provided for the weak so they do not lose heart in this work, but let all have help according to the size of the community or the circumstances of the place" (RB 35.3-4). Now we see the other side of the coin: the brothers should serve one another, but they should not be overburdened. If they need help to do their service, they should get it. Clearly, this is another good principle for healthy common life: people should get the help they need. And that seems to imply that they will let the superiors know when they need help. We cannot expect the superiors to know everything!

It is perhaps worth noting that Benedict uses a very specific term in regard to the help that the "weak" should get when they need it: *solacium* means concrete help, not just verbal encouragement. If our work crew is understaffed, then it does not help much for the superior to give us a pep talk. What we want is more workers! The Latin word that I have translated here by "lose heart" is our old friend *tristitia*. It seems apparent to me that we are looking here at the problem of discouragement, which is a serious form of sadness. Benedict does not want his monks to succumb to dejection, since it is not good for their souls, and it is also not good for the monastery economy.

When I read verses like these, I am mindful of that case in the Jewish Bible where King Rehoboam, when he takes over for his father Solomon, is petitioned by the northern tribes to lighten their tax burden, and also their labor burden. Rehoboam consults his advisors, who are also young men like himself. Their advice? Tell them: "My father chastised you with whips, but I will chastise you with scorpions [heavier whips]!" (1 Kgs 12:11). Not only did he crush the hopes of the people, but he provoked a revolt. From that day on, the ten northern tribes seceded from the Jewish union. Rehoboam found out the consequences of denying the people *solacium*!

Someone who knows the Benedictine Rule well might at this point interject: What about murmuring? Are we not forbidden to indulge in it? Yes, we are, but as much as Benedict dislikes murmuring, he also knows that some murmuring is simply justified. In fact, When discussing the daily diet with regard to when the monks eat and how much they are fed, Benedict says that if the workload is heavy, they must be fed earlier and better. Otherwise, he says, they will react with *justifiable* murmuring (RB 41.5). In a case like that, the monks have a right to complain since they are not being properly taken care of. It is the abbot's job to supply the community with necessities. As Benedict puts it in RB 55.20-22:

> The abbot should ponder the verse from the Acts of the Apostles: "Each person used to receive what was necessary" (Acts 4:35). So the abbot should pay attention to the weaknesses of the needy and not the bad will of the envious. But in all his decisions, he should remember the judgment of God.

Chapter 13

Timetable

In this chapter we will focus our attention on RB 48, which is concerned with the timetable of the monastery. We have already noted that Benedict generally breaks free of his dependence on the Rule of the Master after the first few chapters. But in this case, fairly late in the Rule, he again seems to base himself on that prototype (RM 50). In both cases they structure their remarks on the horarium itself, describing what should take place at the third hour, the sixth hour, the ninth hour, and so on. But even a casual glance reveals that the Master carries this program out in far greater detail than Benedict. And we will also see that these two authors fill in the details in very different ways. At any rate, this comparison aids us greatly in exploring the riches of RB 48.

One difference is immediately evident: RB 48 is only one-third as long as RM 50. That means that Benedict has greatly abridged his model. In fact, this scale of abridgement matches that of the whole RB, which is only one-third as long as RM. We do not know why Benedict chose to produce a much shorter Rule, but I think we should conclude that he deliberately eliminated much material that did not suit his purposes. It is a temptation, and one that some famous exegetes like Adalbert de Vogüé do not avoid, to fill in the blank spots of RB with the fullness of RM. I consider this an unwarranted move.

Busyness and Sin

Someone who bothers to read RM 50 itself (translated by Luke Eberle in Cistercian Studies 6) will notice a very curious thing. Every three hours the monks gather for a short prayer (Prime, Terce, Sext, and None). That breaks up the work day, but it is thoroughly traditional: all the ancient monasteries did this. What is not traditional, however, is the explanation that the Master gives as to *why* they gather so often:

> And when they have with due decorum completed these further three hours in silent labor, let them hasten to the divine praises at Sext, giving thanks to the Lord in the oratory for having been entitled again to spend another three hours of the day occupied in silent labor free from sin. (RM 50.22-23)

The last three words are crucial: "free from sin." This is not an offhand remark by the Master but a *leitmotif*, for he repeats it for each of the Day Hours. Not only that, at the very center of his elaborately structured chapter, at RM 50.37-38, he expands a bit on this refrain:

> The deans are to keep watch over the brothers at all times so that no brother is completely idle. For when he is occupied in doing something he has no time to think of anything except what he is intent upon doing with his hands. (RM 50.37-38)

This is no casual remark, but a basic principle of the Master's thinking. He is convinced that monks have to be kept busy so they do not fall into mischief or, worse, into sin. In this sense, the Master shows himself to be a sort of proto-Calvinist a thousand years before the Geneva reformer.

In his classic book *The Protestant Ethic and the Spirit of Capitalism* (1930), the German sociologist Max Weber tied the capitalist exaltation of hard work to the Calvinist countries. Those people, mostly northern Europeans, found Calvin's doctrine of predestination unbearable. To keep their minds off the question "am I predestined for heaven or hell?" the Calvinist pastors advised them to simply keep busy; don't think about it! Is this what the Master is doing? To judge from some of his comments, it must be so. Consider the following:

> While the brother is engaged in some task he fixes his eyes on his work and thereby occupies his attention with what he is doing, and

has no time to think about anything else, and is not submerged in a flood of desires. Absentmindedness does not bring blankness to his eyes when hand and attention are occupied doing something. (RM 50.2-5)

This is the way the Master leads off his chapter 50, so there is no doubt about his thinking. He is in the business of busyness! Keep 'em busy!

As for Benedict, he does not seem to buy into this gospel of activism. For example, he never characterizes the Day Hours as services of thanksgiving for "having avoided sin for three more hours." He has completely eliminated this sin-obsessed mantra. This does not mean Benedict is unconcerned with sin; he is just not obsessed with it. Furthermore, he has replaced the Master's wordy lead-off quote with a single sentence: "Idleness is the soul's enemy."

This punchy little aphorism, which is mistakenly attributed to St. Basil by *RB 1980*, was widely quoted in ancient times. As a general rule for mental and spiritual health it is helpful enough, but the temptation is to fill it in with the abundance of our own preoccupations, or with the dubious doctrine of the Rule of the Master. Although the aphorism has a certain importance for Benedict (it is, after all, a programmatic statement), it should not be expanded into a Benedictine motto for furious activity.

Free for *Lectio*

A strong clue, and one of many, that Benedict does not share the Master's preoccupation with busywork lies in the remarkable terms that he uses to describe *lectio divina*. Over and over, he says: "Let them be free for *lectio*" (*lectioni vacent*). I think it is much more than curious that the traditional translation of this phrase was always: "Let them devote themselves to *lectio*." I must admit that good Latin dictionaries give "devote oneself" as a transferred, but rare, meaning for *vacare*. But it seems to me that the whole tenor of Benedict's approach to *lectio* is in the direction of "free for."

A comparison with the *practice* as well as the vocabulary of RM 50 can show us why. For the Master, *lectio divina* is essentially a group activity. In RM 50.10-15 we are given a charming picture of the monks at *lectio*. What are they doing? They are gathered in little groups listening to the reading of the Scriptures. By repetition, the group is expected to learn these passages by heart. Then later the individuals come before a kind of examining board and repeat what they have learned. This is very much like the way that boys still learn the Qur'an in the mosques of the Middle East. The Master describes this as "the work of the spirit," which can be interpreted in several ways. But it does sound very much like *work*. Benedict sets aside some time after the night Office (RB 8.3) for "learning the psalms and lessons," which I understand as memorizing parts for the Divine Office, but that is not *lectio*.

Benedict's monks do not gather in small groups for *lectio divina*. They may have done this as young boys to learn how to read, but as adult monks they do *lectio* by themselves. Of course, we know they did not have private rooms, but it seems they could usually find a place alone in the cloister area (outdoors!). Like the monks of the Master, they probably spent most of their *lectio* time with the Bible, but they spent it in a rather different way than as "work of the spirit."

The main "work" of doing *lectio* was not memorization; it was "rumination." That term, which reminds us of cows and other animals that "chew the cud," refers to pondering that which has been memorized. It no doubt means the slow, careful consideration of the biblical text itself. But it is probably not very helpful to characterize this as "work." Probably "contemplation" would be a more accurate word.

This does not mean that *lectio* was, and is, easy! To say that it is not exactly "work" does not mean that it is not strenuous. For one thing, Benedict wants us to do quite a bit of it, as much as three hours some seasons of the year. By any standard, that is a goodly chunk of the monastic day. It is by no means just a few minutes tucked in here and there. Indeed, it is so considerable that apparently the ancient monks sometimes found it burdensome. If we doubt this, listen to the following:

> Above all, one or two seniors should surely be assigned to patrol the monastery at the times when the brothers are free for *lectio*. They should be on the lookout for the bored brother who gives himself

over to frivolity or gossip and is not serious about *lectio*. Not only
is he useless to himself, but he leads others astray as well. If such a
one be found out—perish the thought!—let him be admonished once
and again a second time. If he does not improve, he should undergo
the regular correction in such a way that others will be afraid. Nor
should the brothers fraternize at improper times. (RB 48.17-21)

This is a precious window into the actual *reality* of ancient *lectio*.
At the risk of repetition: it was not easy! Why are some monks
trying to get out of it? If they are "free for *lectio*," then apparently
they are not finding this particular kind of freedom too pleasant.
Perhaps a clue to the problem here lies in the term *acediosus*, which
I have translated "bored" in the quote given above. Often the term
is translated "lazy," but I am pretty sure that gives the wrong idea.

Spiritual Laziness = *Acedia*

For one thing, Latin has several words for "lazy" (*piger*, *ignavus*,
segnis, *iners*) but *acediosus* is not one of them. The fact is that there
are different kinds of laziness, and the one we usually mean is *physically lazy*. But that does not seem to be the issue in RB 48.17-21.
Here the monks are expected to engage in *lectio divina*, which is not
essentially a physical activity, and certainly not a strenuous physical
one. It would seem that the brother who finds *lectio* difficult, or
perhaps even impossible, is not physically lazy but rather "bored."
This is corroborated by Benedict's remarks on the Sunday schedule
at the end of RB 48:

> On Sunday all should be free for *lectio*, except for those who are
> assigned to various tasks. But if someone is so negligent and slothful
> that he will not or cannot meditate or read, he should be assigned
> some work to keep him busy. As for sick or fragile brothers, they
> should be assigned a work or craft so that they will be engaged
> but not so crushed by heavy labor that they flee. The abbot must
> remain aware of their weakness. (RB 48.22-23)

First, I must admit that I may have contributed to the confusion by
my translation of "slothful" (1996). The Latin word Benedict uses

here is *desidiosus*. Now this word resembles *acediosus*, but I am not sure it has precisely the same flavor. When we see "slothful" we usually think of physical laziness, but again I doubt if this is the point here. After all, Benedict recommends that the *desidiosi* be given physical work—on Sunday! He sees this as somehow a cure for what ails them. But what *does* ail them?

Getting back to the term *acediosus*, I find it hard to ignore the resemblance of this adjective with *acedia*. Now *acedia* is definitely a loaded word in early monastic vocabulary. What is it? To attempt a short and sweet definition is difficult, but suffice it to say that *acedia* is not simple physical laziness. Rather, it is a technical term used by the Greek monks to refer to *spiritual torpor* or *lassitude*.

A monk afflicted with *acedia* was one who found himself unable to respond with enthusiasm to the things of the spirit or the things of God. No doubt "boredom" is a better English equivalent than laziness, but neither one carries the precise connotation of *acedia*. It must be admitted that some of the Fathers, like John Cassian, recommended physical labor as an antidote to *acedia*, but that does not mean they thought of it as physical fatigue. Rather, it was the much more subtle and difficult condition of lack of spiritual zest. Perhaps a common enough modern equivalent would be lack of gratitude to God for who I am and what I have. But we cannot pursue this particular rabbit too far into the brush.

Fine-Tuning or Fussiness?

When studying the monastic timetable that Benedict presents in RB 48, we may have noticed how "fussy" he is. For example, take the first verse: "From Easter till the first of October, they should go out from Prime in the morning and work until *almost* the fourth hour" (*usque hora paene quarta*). Why "almost"? Why not just the fourth hour? We really don't know, but it should be noted that this kind of minor adjustment occurs in almost every stage of the horarium. Why must Benedict make these constant little adjustments?

The difference with the Rule of the Master is very evident when one lays them side by side. For the Master, things must happen exactly on the hour. Terce comes precisely at the third hour (nine o'clock in the morning), sext comes exactly at noon, and none comes right at three o'clock. In a certain sense, one cannot fault the Master for his fidelity to the "correct" canonical hours. Historically speaking, the Master is in perfect harmony with the rest of the early monastic lawgivers—except Benedict! They all want things to happen at the exact hour they should happen.

In itself, this is no bad thing. After all, Benedict too wants things to be what they are called. For example, "The abbot who is worthy of ruling a monastery ought always to remember what he is called [*abbas* = father]" (RB 2.1). "The oratory should be in fact what it is called [prayer-room], and nothing else should be done or stored there" (RB 52.1). With regard to the celebration of the canonical hours of the Divine Office, history shows us what happens when we play too fast and loose with this principle. When I first came to the monastery, we sometimes found ourselves celebrating Vespers at noon and Vigils at five o'clock in the evening! There were reasons for this, but the church no longer condones this kind of massive "adjustment."

So then what are we to make of Benedict's penchant for slightly readjusting the hours of the Office, or at least the Day Hours? We don't know exactly why he made any of these minor changes, but I think we can assume he did it "for the good of the order." We can guess that he found from experience that things had to be slid forward or backward a bit because of the very human needs of the brothers. For example, in RB 48.6 he wants "None is to be recited early, about the middle of the eighth hour." I think we can guess why: because the brothers are ravenously hungry! Remember that this is their first meal of the day. By three o'clock in the afternoon they may be fainting from hunger; therefore he moves the meal up half an hour.

At this point I can't help thinking of Jesus himself. When he was chided by his critics because his disciples were "harvesting" on the Sabbath, he retorted, "The Sabbath was made for man, not man for the Sabbath; the Son of Man is also lord of the Sabbath" (Mark 2:27-28). At the deepest level, Jesus is here declaring himself above the Sabbath regulations. But on a more general level, he is also criticizing the Pharisees for clinging to a very rigid interpretation of the law of Sabbath rest. In his estimation, they were using the law in an inhumane fashion, but it had been instituted to promote human life, not cripple it.

An incident from the history of my own monastery comes to mind here. For a long time the community has sung the First Vespers of Sunday at 5:10 on Saturday evening. Now there is also a parish liturgy at four o'clock that usually ends about 4:50, so there is no conflict. But once in a while, the parish Mass does not end quite "on time" and this prevents the monks from processing into church and their choir stalls right on time. They may have to wait five minutes. The abbot at the time was quite bothered by all this. He knew very well that the pastor could not absolutely guarantee that the parish Mass would be over by 4:50. On the other hand, he did not want to alter the monastic schedule in the slightest. So he fussed and fumed.

Here was a textbook example of "man being made for the Sabbath." The monastic schedule, which is an essentially arbitrary thing, had become in the abbot's mind some kind of law written in stone, not to be tinkered with. Hence, an abstract principle was allowed to predominate, even though he could have easily adjusted things to avoid any conflict. Granted, it is not good to be constantly fiddling with the horarium. It confuses people, and it can also irritate them. But when a slight adjustment can serve to make life easier and less conflictual, then we ought to do it. Benedict did it often enough in RB 48!

Position as Emphasis

Since we are trying to uncover some of the significance of RB 48 by comparing it to RM 50, we might also notice the overall arrangement of the discussion. When the Master comes to discuss the schedule, he first turns to winter, which for him means the period from the twenty-fourth of September until Easter. This means that the penitential seasons of Advent and Lent come under discussion first; only later does the Master discuss Easter time, which, in the Christian ethos, is essentially a time for rejoicing.

For his part, Benedict turns the tables by discussing the Easter season and summer first; only then does he turn to the penitential time of winter and Lent. Benedict does not make a big thing about this change in procedure, but sometimes the *obiter acta*, the causal, offhand acts, may tell us more than the explicit ones. It could well be that Benedict wants to emphasize Easter and its aftermath more than Advent and Lent, which are, after all, liturgically preparatory and not ultimate. For Christians, Easter is the main feast because theologically the resurrection of Jesus Christ is the foundation of everything else. To put it another way, and to cite Adalbert de Vogüé, Easter is the ultimate criterion for Benedict.

When discussing the arrangement of the horarium, we cannot ignore the place of the physical seasons. They are not as important as the liturgical seasons, but they are not negligible either. In the northern hemisphere, where both RM and RB were no doubt written, wintertime is colder than summertime. In response to this, the Master arranges for *lectio divina* in the early morning "because it is cold and the brothers cannot do any work in the morning" (RM 50.9). This seems reasonable and even humane, but notice the implication: the Master has *lectio* done when nothing else can be done! It is a kind of fill-in for work, which must be somehow more important than *lectio* for him.

Benedict, for his part, seems to choose better times for *lectio*. He discreetly drops the remark about it being too cold in winter; he has *lectio* first thing in the morning because that is the best time for it, at least in my opinion. I have to admit, however, that this is not the only arrangement for Benedict. In the summer, he wants the monks to go out for field work first thing in the morning. *Lectio* only comes about ten o'clock in the morning and then again after the main meal. These are not ideal times, but in the Mediterranean region it is simply too hot at midday to work outdoors. Sensible people reserve that time to siesta and a leisurely dinner.

With the mention of leisure, we return to a key question with regard to the monastic life. What is the role of leisure for the monk? We noted earlier that Benedict has an aversion to the idea of *otiositas*, which is idleness. That could lead us, incorrectly, to assume that he is not much interested in *otium*, which is a very different thing. *Otium* means precisely leisure, and it was a major concern for religious people in ancient times. It is true that Benedict does not explicitly set aside any time for what we now call recreation. Does that mean he has no interest in the reality that everyone needs some free time, some leisure? I doubt that very much. Compared to some of the other ancient rules and writers, he is much less determined that the monks work hard all day long.

One monastic legislator from Benedict's era, or a little earlier, was the famous Augustine of Hippo. Augustine was from the upper classes, not the peasantry, so he shared with the aristocracy a high valuation for *otium*. In fact, when writing about his monastic foundation in North Africa (Thagaste), he proudly describes the monks as engaging in contemplative leisure: *deificari in otio*. This is a truly pregnant phrase for Augustine: "To become godlike in leisure." This was his main purpose in organizing, and living, monastic life. True, he was soon called away to be a busy bishop, but he knew that the use of leisure was crucial for a Christian contemplative.

Although St. Benedict never speaks of *deificari in otio*, I am quite sure he knew what it meant. Otherwise, he would not have set aside so much time for *lectio divina*. Taken in addition to the Divine Office, *lectio divina* really amounts to the main occupation of the monk. Of course, we have to make a living and so we have to engage in profitable work. But the monastery is never a factory. Some historians claim the Pachomian communities were primarily organized for work, but that is simply not true. (See *Pachomian Koinonia, passim*, trans. A. Veilleux). No. Monks are meant "to become godly in leisure."

Chapter 14

Priesthood

To study the topic of priesthood in the Rule, and indeed in all of ancient monasticism, is to come up against some surprising facts. First of all, the earliest monks were mostly laymen. In fact, it was typical that they had to go into the nearest village for Mass on Sunday. This being the case, it is not surprising that they did not have daily Mass, as is found in Catholic monasteries today. Further, it is often suggested that St. Benedict himself was not a priest. We can't be sure about this, but at least there is the intriguing comment in RB 62.1: "If any abbot needs to have a priest ordained for himself, he should choose from among his monks one worthy of the sacerdotal office." That certainly sounds like the abbot himself was not a priest.

Nowadays very few monasteries of men have no priest, but *all* female monasteries are in this situation. Of course, women have never been ordained in the Catholic Church, but nuns were usually able to find a chaplain. Now, however, in some places there is an acute shortage of priests, leaving the nuns in a serious bind. In some cases, daily Mass is no longer available to them, and even on Sundays they may have to go out to the parish church. Obviously, we cannot solve that problem here, but perhaps some background will aid understanding.

When we survey the monastic literature prior to Benedict, we don't find much comment on priests. We hear that the first cenobitic founder, Pachomius of Egypt, refused ordination when the patriarch Saint Athanasius offered it to him (SBo 25). The bishop wanted to make sure the monks had Mass, but Pachomius thought that priesthood could cause pride in monks. Eventually, though, he accepted priests into his monastery because then the monks would not have to go out for Mass. The other great cenobitic founder, Basil of Caesarea, soon became the bishop of the region, so we can assume he found ways to supply liturgy for his monasteries.

Saint Augustine of Hippo is an interesting case regarding the priesthood. When he founded his monastery at Thagaste, it was composed of laymen as usual. But fairly soon Augustine was roped into ordination by the bishop of Hippo and against his better judgment became himself the next bishop of that city in North Africa. He founded another monastery at Hippo but did not live in it because he felt his presence as bishop would be a distraction to the monks. It is interesting that when he wrote his rule for monks, the so-called *Praeceptum*, he arranged for a dual superior: the house prior would be a layman, but there would also be a nonresident priest to oversee the community. Since this monastery was in the garden of the cathedral, there was no worry about liturgy for the monks.

The Rule of the Master

When we turn to the Rule of the Master, St. Benedict's general prototype, we suddenly find that priesthood has become a major issue. The surprising, perhaps shocking, fact is that the Master refuses to allow priests into his community. In RM 77.3-4, we get a hint of his negative feeling about priests: if they visit the monks, they must *give* blessings, but never *receive* blessings from the monks. Clearly, the Master makes a sharp distinction between these two states of life.

In RM 83 the Master goes on to elaborate his thinking on this subject. The chapter begins very strongly: "Priests are to be considered outsiders in the monastery, especially those who retain and exercise their presidency and preferment in churches." Lest there be any doubt about the implications of this, if priests visit a monastery (that is, the Master's monastery!), they needn't think they automatically become important. "Nothing is to be permitted them in the monasteries other than praying the collects, saying the conclusion, and giving the blessing." These things are *permitted* them; they are not theirs by right of their priesthood.

We might pause a moment here to notice the phrase "saying the conclusion." The Latin is saying the *missas*. This term fooled translators here (and in the Rule of Benedict) for a long time. It certainly looks like "saying Mass," but that is not what it means. In fact, the term *missa* for sixth-century Christians meant the closing prayer of a service. We had a trace of this in the closing of Mass itself up until the reform of 1970: *Ite, missa est!* which came to mean "Go, the Mass is ended." It really meant "Go, this is the end!" At any rate, scholars used to think that this somehow meant that the monks had daily Mass. In fact, they did not; they had daily Communion. That was the case with the Rule of the Master (RM 22) and also with the Rule of Benedict (RB 38.2).

Even though the Master allows priests to visit the monastery, and even for long periods of time, he is uneasy with them. He wants them to know that they are not to expect privileged treatment but must instead join in the common labor with the brothers. If they refuse to work, or if they misbehave in any other way, they are to be physically expelled. Apparently, the Master has no illusions about the angelic nature of all priests. But the main worry for the Master with regard to priests is that they may be tempted to *usurp the abbot's power and authority*. In fact, we have documentary evidence of that very thing from the decrees of Pope Gregory the Great later in the same sixth century.

There is a very curious passage in the Rule of the Master that could lie behind some of the author's extreme anxiety about sacerdotal pretensions. Near the end of the long, flamboyant RM 1 on the kinds of monks, the Master makes an attempt to create ecclesiastical categories. Here we quote RM 1.82-83: "Now, the Lord has given his church, in conformity with the Trinity, three series of teaching: first, that of prophets; second, that of apostles; third, that of teachers [*doctores*]." Quoting but reworking 1 Corinthians 12:28, the Master claims that the leaders of the Great Church are the prophets and apostles. But the third category, the teachers, says the Master, are in charge of "sheepfolds," that is, monasteries.

Now it has to be said that this ecclesiology, clever and creative as it appears, is in fact bogus. It involves a splintering of 1 Corinthians 12:28, and it also claims something that the church never has accepted. The problem is that it appears to set the abbot on par with the bishop. To the Master, they are both somehow successors of the leaders of the early church. But in fact the New Testament and the church has no such place for abbots or any other leaders of religious orders. To put it in somewhat formal terms, abbots and all monks are part of the "charismatic" church; bishops are the leaders of the institutional church. In no sense are they equal in power or function. Abbots are strictly *under* the bishops.

Still, the church understands that there can be such a thing as *clerical encroachment.* There can be situations where the institutional church tries to manage the charismatic church, to the detriment of the latter. This happens (rarely now) in the case of nuns, where the superior may seem to have even less spiritual power than a male superior. But in fact the case is the same: the bishop has no spiritual power over the nun (or monk) *as such.* That belongs to the abbot or prioress. Of course, extreme cases of abbatial malfunction may necessitate the intervention of the local bishop.

The Rule of Benedict

The attitude of Saint Benedict toward priests is somewhat the same as that of his literary model, the Master, but it is also different. Unlike the Master, Benedict does admit priests who wish to join his community. RB 60, which is entirely devoted to this matter, starts out thus: "If any ordained priest asks to be received into the monastery, do not agree too quickly" (RB 60.1). If that is not exactly a ringing endorsement, at least it is not a complete prohibition.

But the rest of RB 60 mostly consists of warnings to the priest-become-monk that things will not be made easy for him because of his status as a priest. In case he is thinking otherwise, we hear this stern warning: "He must recognize that he will have to observe the full discipline of the Rule without any mitigation" (RB 60.2-3). The full force of this caveat hit the priest right away in the novitiate where he would be thrown together with the young men who just came from the "world" or perhaps those who had been *oblates* since their childhood. That kind of treatment must have been a shock for even the humblest priest! To tell the truth, however, few monasteries carried out this tough measure in full: priests were usually accorded some special consideration.

As we have already seen, Benedict not only accepted priestly candidates; he also had some of his monks ordained. RB 62, which is dedicated to the "priests of the monastery," is much like RB 60 in that it consists mostly of anxious warning against priestly pretensions: "The monk so ordained must be on guard against conceit or pride, must not presume to do anything except what the abbot commands him, and must recognize that now he will have to subject himself all the more to the discipline of the Rule" (RB 62.2-3). In the light of these dire warnings, it is a wonder that any of the old monks dared to present themselves for ordination. Yet we should also remember that it was usually out of obedience that they did so; they were *asked* by the abbot and the community to become priests, for the community needed their ministry.

Moreover, RB 62 ends with a paragraph of material that should have been enough to scare the wits out of a prospective monk-priest. What if a such a priest, despite all these warnings, nevertheless steps out of line or, even worse, refuses to obey? "If after many warnings he does not improve, let the bishop too be brought in as a witness. Should he not amend even then, and his faults become notorious, he is to be dismissed from the monastery, but only if he is so arrogant that he will not submit or obey the Rule" (RB 62.9-11).

It seems to me that this barrage of hesitations and prohibitions must have had their source in painful experience for Benedict. If he had not been burned by hard experiences with arrogant priests, I doubt if he would have indulged himself in such a torrent of negative comments. Probably one or more of the humble monks he had ordained turned out to be not so humble after all! Perhaps the priesthood, with its aura of sanctity and holy power, had turned monastic heads and made them pompous clerical prigs. Such things have not been unknown in the long history of monasticism.

An abbot I know told me that one of his monks was assigned to a parish nearby. After a year or two, he came to the abbot and asked permission for a long vacation to his home in Eastern Europe. When the abbot asked him about the cost, the monk assured him that he had saved up enough money for the trip. The astonished abbot asked him if he had been sending in his salary to the procurator, but the monk said he thought the money was his. When the abbot admonished him about this, the monk-priest grew increasingly belligerent and eventually left the monastery. Benedict does not take such things for granted.

Priesthood in Benedictine History

Someone who knows only present-day Benedictines might be surprised by the troubled early history of the priests in the monastery. Nowadays, priesthood is no exception in our monasteries; indeed, it can be said that worldwide, *most* Benedictine monks are priests. And what is more, this has been the case throughout most of Benedictine history! How did we get from the rather sour worries of the Master and Benedict to the present situation? How did we get from no priests, or very few priests, to the legions of priests we find in some big monasteries?

As a matter of fact, the change came rather soon after the time of Saint Benedict. We know that by the year 800, in other words 250 years after Benedict, most monks were being ordained priests. We know this from the written *Lives* of the monks but also and especially from archeology. The floorplans of the elaborate monastic churches that were being built in the ninth century, churches such as Saint Riquier near Abbeville, had multiple "side-altars," as many as fifteen or twenty! These secondary altars were not merely ornamental; they were used for daily Masses. But not ordinary Masses—private Masses. That is, Masses celebrated by a priest alone, accompanied by a server.

What was this all about? It was about the new devotion to daily Masses dedicated to specific patrons. In the early Middle Ages, people got into the habit of donating small (or large) sums of money to priests and monasteries to have Masses said for the souls of the faithful departed. Rich people often set aside a good deal of money to have Masses said every day for themselves after death, presumably to promote them from purgatory to heaven. But, of course, this new devotional situation had important side effects, and one of them was the necessity of ordaining more monks to the priesthood. Most medieval monks celebrated at least one private Mass a day for the souls of the faithful departed.

Moreover, this situation was by no means ephemeral. When I entered the monastery in 1956, my own house, which had about eighty monks, had at least fifteen side-altars in the main church and also in side chapels. Typically, at least one or two Masses were said on each altar per day, beginning early in the morning during Matins. Since each of these Masses also needed a server, that meant that most of the monks were either celebrating private Masses or serving at them. In those days, private Masses were a very important part of the daily regime of the average Benedictine monastery.

How did this all come about? The origins may not be entirely clear, but it seems they go back to that *fons et origo* of most things Catholic, namely, the city of Rome. Everybody knows that Rome is full of churches, but what they may not know is that Rome is also full of processions, or at least it used to be. Even today there are still what are called stational churches where during Lent special Masses are held. More than that, each stational church has a sister-church where the clergy and the faithful start out the liturgy for the day. For example, on Ash Wednesday, the pope himself always comes to Sant'Anselmo, the Benedictine church, where he vests; then he and the faithful walk down the street a block to Santa Sabina, the Dominican church, for Mass.

What has this got to do with private Masses in northern Europe? Simply this: the German and French Catholics were keen on imitating the liturgy in Rome. Instead of building station-churches, they built multiple altars in their big abbey churches, and they loved to process from one altar to another. The monks at Cluny, which had the largest church in Christendom, spent hours every day walking in formal procession from private altar to private altar. By doing that, they felt they were virtually living in Rome.

Monastic Implications of Multiple Masses and Private Masses

We would not be spending so much time on this topic here if it did not have a good deal of impact on monastic thinking and practice. A moment's thought will tell us why. The introduction of multiple priests in a monastery is bound to have an effect on the community. For one thing, they will probably not be content with the simple work that Benedict's original monks performed. Priest-monks need a good deal of education, and once they have it, they want to use it. That means they usually want to teach in a seminary or a college, or at least function as parish priests.

Medieval monks did not live and work in parishes as do many modern monks. They said private Masses in the monastery. But over the course of time there was pressure for the monks to care for parishes apart from the monastery. The result, at least in the United States with its vast distances, was and is to take monk-priests out of the monastery. Indeed, it has not been unusual for a given monk-priest to be assigned to distant parishes for his entire monastic life. Recently, one of my confreres returned to the monastery after forty-one years on a Native American mission! During that time, we rarely saw him. Since he spent most of his time driving around his vast parish, no wonder when he "came home" he continued to drive around as long as he could.

One of the important aspects of multiple Masses and multiple priests is what is called Mass stipends. Put briefly, people give us a good deal of money earmarked for Masses. We do not like to say we are *paid to say Mass*, but it does come to that. It would not be honest to claim that this source of revenue is unimportant for us. In fact, it is important for the whole church. As long as Catholics are willing to contribute in this way, it will help to support the monastery. But the secularization of modern life does not augur well for Mass stipends. Enough said.

Probably the most important element of daily Masses for a monastery has to do with the horarium. We must set aside about an hour a day for the community Mass, and obviously this affects our whole schedule. People sometimes complain that modern monasteries no longer carry out the full Divine Office as Benedict lays it out in his Rule. What they fail to notice is that Benedict set aside *no time* for daily Mass. In fact, there were no daily Masses in his day. People only prayed Mass on Sunday. But if Benedict would have wanted to insert daily Mass in his horarium, it would have seriously impacted the whole horarium.

It is true that very few priests still say private Masses. The norm nowadays is a concelebrated community Mass, with most of the priests of the community celebrating jointly. Most liturgists, and most ordinary monks as well, consider this a vast improvement over the old system. To have a dozen priests saying private Masses simultaneously in the same church now seems rather bizarre. We used to do it without batting an eye, but to tell the truth it always was somewhat grotesque. To make it worse, in the "good old days" all the servers were required to leave "their priest" and rush to the abbot's Mass for Communion. It was a strange sight to say the least, but of course much that we do today will also seem odd in the future.

Actually, concelebrated community Mass has other important ramifications as well. In most monasteries, it means that the priests rotate as main minister, which gives them all a chance to preach to their confreres. This was something that was almost unknown in the old regime. The only one who preached to the community was the abbot, and he did so only on major feast days. In my monastery, the monks rarely heard a sermon at all! Hard as this is to imagine and understand, we took it for granted; we did not reflect on how strange it all was. Of course, private Masses *never* had a sermon, but neither did the so-called conventual Mass. The Trappists had sermons in the Chapter, but we Benedictines did not.

When I write like this about monastic sermons, or rather the lack of them, it may sound strange. It may sound like I love them. In fact, I love some of them, and some of them I do not love. Sermons, or homilies, as we now call them, can either be a great source of edification—or a terrible source of irritation. One of the typical sins against common sense committed by monastic celebrants is long, boring homilies at weekday Mass. When the priest cannot stay under five minutes, we have a problem. It is much harder to give a good short homily than a poor long one. Daily Mass should not normally run forty-five minutes. When it does, the monastic horarium is in danger of distortion.